PER

I0672750

AGAINST WORRY

TYNDALE HOUSE PUBLISHERS, INC.,
CAROL STREAM, ILLINOIS

O
V
VE
VER
VERW
VERWH
VERWHE
VERWHEL
VERWHELM
VERWHELME
VERWHELMED
VERWHELMED
VERWHELMED
VERWHELMED
VERWHELMED

Visit Tyndale online at www.tyndale.com.

Visit the author's website at www.perrynoble.com.

TYNDALE and Tyndale's quill logo are registered trademarks of Tyndale House Publishers, Inc.

Overwhelmed: Winning the War against Worry

Copyright © 2014 by Perry Noble. All rights reserved.

Edited by Stephanie Rische

Published in association with Yates & Yates (www.yates2.com).

Unless otherwise indicated, all Scripture quotations are taken from the *Holy Bible*, New Living Translation, copyright © 1996, 2004, 2007, 2013 by Tyndale House Foundation. Used by permission of Tyndale House Publishers, Inc., Carol Stream, Illinois 60188. All rights reserved.

Scripture quotations marked NIV are taken from the Holy Bible, *New International Version,*® *NIV.*® Copyright © 1973, 1978, 1984, 2011 by Biblica, Inc.™ Used by permission of Zondervan. All rights reserved worldwide. www.zondervan.com.

Library of Congress Cataloging-in-Publication Data
Noble, Perry.
  Overwhelmed : winning the war against worry / Perry Noble.
      pages cm
  Includes bibliographical references.
  ISBN 978-1-4143-6886-3 (sc)
  1. Worry—Religious aspects—Christianity. 2. Stress management—Religious aspects—Christianity. I. Title.
  BV4908.5.N63 2014
  248.8'6—dc23   2013044080

Printed in the United States of America

20	19	18	17	16	15	14
7	6	5	4	3	2	1

I would like to dedicate this book to my wife, Lucretia. All through my battle with depression and anxiety, you stood by my side, encouraged me, and supported me. You are God's gift to me, and it is my prayer that I will always view you through the eyes of Jesus.

CONTENTS

THE BATTLEFIELD OF THE MIND

I wanted to kill myself.

No, that isn't just a figure of speech or an attempt to be overly dramatic. I honestly couldn't get away from the idea that the only way to escape my pain, confusion, and frustration was to take my own life.

At first it was just a passing thought. I was driving home one day, and I distinctly remember looking at a stoplight and thinking, *My light is green—maybe someone who's coming from the other direction will run the light and slam into my car, and my life will be over.*

At that point I sort of snapped back into reality, but from that moment on, similar thoughts would invade my mind every time life threw another overwhelming circumstance at me. I was plagued with thoughts like *You need to just end it all* and *You will never have any relief from this.*

The idea of doing something so drastic seemed to come out of nowhere. I was a pastor at a growing, vibrant church; I was married to the woman of my dreams; I had a beautiful daughter who loved me; we lived in a nice house and didn't have any debt; and I was healthier than I'd ever been. No one who looked at me from the outside would have been able to tell that I'd nearly lost my will to live.

But that was exactly what was happening after years of trying to operate my schedule and responsibilities at an unsustainable pace. Life had finally caught up with me, and I was utterly overwhelmed.

One of the toughest parts about what I was going through was that I didn't think I could tell anyone what I was thinking or how I was feeling because I was afraid people would think I was crazy. So I kept this battle all to myself. As a result, I began to struggle with a whole range of problems.

- Some nights I couldn't sleep . . . even with the assistance of medicine. And as I lay awake, I would worry and obsess over things that were completely out of my control.
- I began to distance myself from people who were close to me.
- I thought about leaving everyone and everything behind and starting all over again.
- I couldn't recall the last time I'd had fun.
- I sank into a deep depression and began having panic attacks.
- Worry became my go-to emotion.
- Everything that happened to me had a dramatic impact on my emotions, whether positive or negative. Emotionally speaking, I was a roller coaster.
- I kept telling myself that what I was going through was simply a season and that once my schedule became less hectic and my responsibilities decreased, I would be fine.

All of us experience stress, anxiety, worry, fear, and depression at some point in our lives. But what I discovered when I was neck deep in this battle was that the church has remained largely silent on this issue. In fact, I've heard church leaders make the declaration that someone who is a Christian and is in right standing with God will never have such struggles.

This is simply not true. Scripture is full of examples of godly people who experienced trials and suffering and overwhelming circumstances through no fault of their own.

If your life seems overwhelming to you right now and you don't know what to do or how to handle it, you are not alone. There are millions of other people who feel trapped in their circumstances and think they can't escape.

So is there a way out of all of this?

Is there a way to reduce the stress and anxiety in our lives so we won't have to walk around in a medicated, zombie-like state of mind?

Is it even possible to experience emotions such as joy and happiness again?

The answer to these questions is yes; however, the journey there isn't quick and easy. There isn't a formula you can pray or a verse you can memorize that will instantly snap you back into a happy place. But I can tell you from personal experience that there *is* a way out, and while it will take a lot of time and energy on your part, it's worth it.

Today I can honestly say I'm more excited and passionate about life than I've ever been. Don't get me wrong—I still wrestle with being overwhelmed. But I now have a much better perspective about how to deal with difficult circumstances when they come my way. My prayer is that after reading this book, you will as well.

Overcoming worry, fear, anxiety, and depression is a journey. I won't be able to offer you three easy steps out of your situation, nor will I share a magical prayer that will suddenly make everything better.

However, I do believe—and it is my prayer—that each chapter of this book will bring you closer to victory—to a place where you are hopeful, not hopeless; peaceful, not anxious; and free, not overwhelmed.

I CAN'T HANDLE THIS!

Several years ago I was a guest speaker at a weeklong event for high school students. Everything was going along as smoothly as you could expect when you have several hundred teenagers all packed into one place . . . until that Thursday I will never forget. I was informed that morning by the leader of the organization that for the afternoon activity we'd all be going tubing.

Before I continue with this story, you have to understand that I may be the biggest doofus on the planet when it comes to anything remotely adventurous. Now don't get me wrong—I like working out and going to the gym, but every time I try something another person claims will be "fun and exciting" (such as snow skiing, waterskiing, or white-water rafting), I always—I mean *always*—get injured. Because of this, anytime someone tells me that "we" are going to try something that involves plummeting from heights, my go-to reaction is most often "You can go eat rocks—there's *no way* I'm getting involved!"

I asked the guy in charge what he meant by tubing, and he kindly explained to me that it was nothing more than sitting in an inner tube and floating down a local creek. "It's one of the most fun, relaxing things on this entire trip," he assured me.

So I agreed to go.

My first clue that this was not going to turn out so well should have come when we arrived at the launching point. The people at the tube rental were informing the camp leader that they had considered shutting down their business for the day because the area had recently received record amounts of rainfall, and as a result, the creek was at flood stage.

The second clue that this was going to end badly was that the "creek" looked much more like a raging river. It was moving so fast that as I got closer to it, I could hardly hear people's voices above the rushing water.

Honestly, I was getting a little stressed; however, I thought, *It's a creek—what's the worst thing that can happen?*

I was about to find out.

My wife, Lucretia, was with me, and she went first on the tubing adventure. The thing you need to understand about my wife is that she is perfect. She was the valedictorian of her high school and college classes. (I beat up our valedictorian.) She went to medical school. She's a second-degree black belt in karate. In short, she is a born winner. So when she set off in her tube, I wasn't surprised to see her head down the creek with a huge smile on her face.

Then it was my turn. So began what I like to refer to as my "three minutes of hell on earth." I sat in the tube and started down the creek. But while my wife had already sped out of sight, my tube seemed to be having issues. Finally I made it over a rock and dropped about three feet—at which point I came flying out of the tube and it continued down the creek without me.

Losing a tube on the creek wasn't a problem. I'd noticed that several other people had been thrown out of their tubes as well due to the water conditions, and I knew that if I could crawl to the creek bank and wait for a few seconds, I'd be able to grab an empty tube that some other poor soul had been flipped out of. I waited no more than ten seconds before I had another tube, thus giving me a renewed opportunity for more fun and excitement.

I plopped down and took off again, experiencing fun and excitement—for about fifteen seconds. Then I abruptly flipped and went under the water. But instead of popping back up to the surface like I had the time before, I got caught in the current of the "creek" and couldn't get myself upright again. I began to wish for things we take for granted in life, such as oxygen, and thought, *So this is how it ends for me. I'm going to die because I drowned in a creek.*

I began grabbing for anything I could find—anything that could pull me out of the current—and I finally managed to get hold of a vine that was connected to the bank. I held on with both hands and pulled with every ounce of strength I had. At last I managed to get my head above the water, and I immediately started gasping and choking, my lungs begging for air.

Eventually I made it out of the creek and collapsed on the bank for quite some time, trying to catch my breath and thanking God that the creek hadn't taken me down. And I can assure you, I didn't get back in that creek again. I staggered and stumbled through the woods until I finally found where our vehicles were parked.

That experience has been on my mind a lot lately as I have prepared to write this book, because it's a tangible reminder of what it feels like to be completely overwhelmed. We climb into college, adulthood, a job, a marriage, or a new endeavor, and we honestly believe it's going to be easy. For crying out loud, we've seen other people do this, and they seem to be just fine.

But before we know it, we've fallen into the creek and feel trapped in the current. We are utterly overwhelmed and can see no way out. As a result, we begin grabbing on to anything we hope might pull us out of the current we're caught up in, which often leads to greater problems instead of helping us.

All of us have been there or perhaps we are there—that place where the current of our circumstances seems to be swirling faster than ever. If we're not prepared, we'll be taken down with it and buy into the lie that insecurity, fear, worry, anxiety, and doubt are the new normal.

But nothing could be further from the truth!

Overwhelmed or Overcoming?

We live in a world that seems to focus on problems, uncertain situations, and the absolutely ridiculous. In the past several weeks I've watched the news at night and heard reports about how our economy is about to go from bad to worse, how solar flares from the sun are going to make airplanes crash, how an asteroid barely missed Earth, and how to survive a zombie attack. (No, I am not making this up!)

Some of those situations are pretty extreme; however, some of the overwhelming situations in life aren't "out there"—they're real and they're right in front of us on a daily basis. Here are just a few of the overwhelming situations you may be up against:

- getting laid off at work
- experiencing struggles in your marriage
- having your first child
- graduating from college with a degree, thousands of dollars' worth of student loans, and no job possibilities in sight
- taking care of aging parents
- getting a call from your doctor saying you need to come in as soon as possible
- not being able to get over a past full of mistakes
- losing someone close to you

I could go on, but I'm sure you get the picture: life can easily become overwhelming!

There are two types of people you don't want to encounter when you're going through something like this. First you have the "that's no big deal" types. You tell them what you're going through and how you're struggling, and their response is, "That's not such a big thing—you need to shut up, quit your crying, and just get over it." Most often they think it isn't a big deal because it's not happening to them. If they were in your shoes, they'd be freaking out too.

Second you have the "let me tell you *my* story" people. You tell them what you're going through and they proceed to insist that your situation pales in comparison to what they've gone through. By the end of a conversation with them, you feel as if you've been emotionally run over by a bus.

I'm going to try not to be either one of these people. Instead, I'm going to share with you some of my own struggles and speak the truth to you—not in a condemning way, but with understanding and practical application.

The first thing I need to say is that your overwhelming circumstances will always be overwhelming, if you allow them to be. In fact, the things that have you worried or stressed right now will most likely not go away by the time you finish reading this book.

Before we go any further, there's a question you must answer honestly: Are you willing to settle for being overwhelmed by circumstances forever, or do you want to step up and overcome whatever is robbing you of joy and life?

> Change begins with a decision: to be overwhelmed or to overcome.

Change begins with a decision: to be overwhelmed or to overcome. Some people never make it out of the current of their circumstances. Instead, they surrender to stress, anxiety, and fear—simply because they don't know how to take the first step out.

Choosing Abundance

The path to victory is paved by making the decision that life is not going to overwhelm you anymore—period. I know this may sound simplistic, but it's true. What gets our attention ultimately determines our direction. If we are constantly focused on our circumstances, we will be overwhelmed.

Let me be very clear. I'm not saying that if you simply think you aren't in bad circumstances, they'll just go away. However, it's a fact that as we shift our focus from our circumstances to Christ, everything in our lives can change. We see this challenge issued to us in the Scriptures over and over again. The author of Hebrews says, "We do this by keeping our eyes on Jesus, the champion who initiates and perfects our faith. Because of the joy awaiting him, he endured the cross, disregarding its shame. Now he is seated in the place of honor beside God's throne" (Hebrews 12:2).

All too often in my battle with fear and anxiety, I kept looking at my situation and my struggles, thinking things would never change, when my focus should have been on my Savior. After all, Jesus died on the cross not only so I wouldn't have to go to hell, but also to give me an abundant life on this earth (see John 10:10).

I know what it's like to live outside of this abundance. I had the incorrect focus for more than three agonizing years, and it resulted in a season of crippling fear, anxiety, worry, and even a dark depression.

I was looking to Jesus to change my circumstances; He was trying to change me.

And He'll do the same for you. It's possible to stop the hamster wheel of feeling overwhelmed day in and day out, and embrace the full, satisfied life Jesus planned for you.

CHAPTER 2

GOD IS GREAT

"God is great, God is good, let us thank Him for our food."

This is the first table blessing I learned to say as a child. I can still remember my mother teaching me this prayer when I was five years old. Every night at the dinner table, she and my dad would bow their heads as I said it, words I took for granted then and didn't live out for many years. It's one thing to say those words, but actually believing them is something completely different.

The temptation when we're feeling overwhelmed is to focus on our problems and circumstances—the issues that got us stuck in the first place. However, when we do that, we give our problems more weight than they deserve, and we end up even more overwhelmed than before.

As crazy as it may seem, the best way to conquer feeling overwhelmed is to take our eyes off what's consuming us and get a bigger picture of what's really important. One of the main ways we accomplish this is by changing our perspective so we can get a true sense of God's character.

The first thing we need to understand about God's character is that He is great, just as it says in the prayer I learned as a child. In the following biblical story, we hear about a guy who truly grasped this concept of God's greatness in the midst of his overwhelming circumstances. But first, let me give you a little historical context.

In 605 BC, Babylon invaded Israel and absolutely laid the smack down, seemingly bringing their nation to an end. And according to historical records from that time period, when one nation conquered another, it was often quite brutal, with thousands of people either getting slaughtered or being forced into slavery.

One of the saddest parts of this tragic situation is that it could have been avoided. The nation of Israel had begun walking away from God hundreds of years earlier, and over and over again He tried to get their attention by sending prophets to try to correct them and set them on the right path. However, they continually refused to listen, and because of their rebellion, He allowed the Babylonians to invade. They arrived with a force unlike anything Israel had ever seen and brought destruction like nothing they'd ever experienced.

This is where we pick up the story in Daniel 1:3-7:

> The king ordered Ashpenaz, his chief of staff, to bring to the palace some of the young men of Judah's royal family and other noble families, who had been brought to Babylon as captives. "Select only strong, healthy, and good-looking young men," he said. "Make sure they are well versed in every branch of learning, are gifted with knowledge and good judgment, and are suited to serve in the royal palace. Train these young men in the language and literature of Babylon." The king assigned them a daily ration of food and wine from his own kitchens. They were to be trained for three years, and then they would enter the royal service.
>
> Daniel, Hananiah, Mishael, and Azariah were four of the young men chosen, all from the tribe of Judah. The chief of staff renamed them with these Babylonian names:
>
> Daniel was called Belteshazzar.
> Hananiah was called Shadrach.
> Mishael was called Meshach.
> Azariah was called Abednego.

One of the things I loved about going to church as a kid was the Bible stories that were taught in Sunday school. The stories of Daniel in the lions' den and of Shadrach, Meshach, and Abednego in the fiery furnace were two that always captured my attention. And this is where these guys are introduced for the first time in Scripture.

Based on what we read in the book of Daniel, along with what we know from history, the Babylonians would invade a nation and then seek the best and brightest young men in the society they'd conquered and try to force these men into a life of slavery. (This is where the story would have ended for me, since I made a 790 on my SAT!)

This scenario of capture and slavery is exactly what was happening to Daniel in this story. One day he was royalty; the next day he was a slave. One day he was on top of the world; the next day he was considered the scum of the earth. Talk about overwhelming circumstances!

After the Babylonians invaded, they likely allowed the poorest people to stay in Israel and work the fields and vineyards; however, they probably killed the others so they wouldn't have to worry about an uprising. Daniel must have seen some of his friends and family members murdered right in front of him at the hands of Babylonians.

Now when I have a bad day, it usually means the batteries in the remote control aren't working, the Internet on my phone is operating incredibly slowly, or the guy at the drive-thru gives me unsweetened tea instead of sweet tea—nothing burns my biscuits quite like that.

But Daniel fared much worse on his bad day.

After killing his fellow countrymen before his very eyes, Daniel's enemies marched him across a couple of deserts from Israel to Babylon (in modern-day Iraq). Then they forced him to change his language, gave him a new wardrobe, and set out to completely change his identity.

I think we can all agree that Daniel was in the middle of some pretty overwhelming circumstances.

Now don't worry—this isn't the point in the book where I tell you that your circumstances are nothing compared to Daniel's and just to be thankful you don't have it as bad as he did. I know the reason you're reading this book is most likely because you're feeling a little stressed or anxious right now, and I don't want to minimize that in any way. What we need to focus on is how Daniel responded to his circumstances. I honestly believe that if we can respond the way he did, we can overcome anything the world throws our way.

Daniel's walk through his overwhelming circumstances to victory began with a decision about what he believed about God. Daniel refused to allow his circumstances to shape his belief system but rather allowed his belief system to help him overcome his circumstances.

The biggest lesson we can learn from Daniel's life is that correct thinking leads to correct actions. Stay with me here while I unpack more of his story.

The Babylonians were trying their best to make Daniel a slave, just as our circumstances often attempt to enslave us. However, we see something near the beginning of the story that changes everything: "Daniel was determined not to defile himself by eating the food and wine given to them by the king. He asked the chief of staff for permission not to eat these unacceptable foods" (Daniel 1:8).

Now I have to admit here that I love food. One of the things that gets me excited about heaven is knowing that, according to the Bible, there's going to be a great feast there. So when I first read this verse, I scratched my head and was a tad confused. In everything Daniel had been through up to this point, he'd just gone along with it. However, when somebody wanted to give him a steak and a glass of wine, *that's* when he was determined not to participate?

> **Correct thinking leads to correct actions.**

But as I dug a little bit deeper into the story and found out more about Babylonian culture, it started making sense. Here's what we read about the food that was served to Daniel: "The king assigned them a daily ration of food and wine from his own kitchens. They were to be trained for three years, and then they would enter the royal service" (Daniel 1:5).

Something to keep in mind was that Babylon was a polytheistic culture, meaning they worshiped many gods. It was quite common for the food and wine that came out of the king's kitchen to have first been put in front of the Babylonian gods as an act of worship. Then, after the food was presented to the gods, it was served to the king and his court.

So in Daniel's case, it wasn't just a matter of trying to be a vegan or being high maintenance by not simply ordering what was on the menu. If you ate the king's food or drank his wine, you were publicly saying, "I am a worshiper of the gods of Babylon."

A line was drawn, and Daniel refused to cross it. It was like he was saying, "You can invade my country, kill my family and friends, march me across a desert, change my name, give me a new language to learn, and force me into a new way of life, but I will *not* acknowledge or worship another god, because my God is greater than the circumstances I am going through."

Despite his overwhelming situation, Daniel kept his eyes focused on God, who he knew was greater than anything he was going through.

That doesn't mean that what Daniel experienced wasn't real or legitimate or that it didn't cause him pain and confusion. But it is obvious from this story that God had Daniel's attention, which is ultimately why he could move toward overcoming rather than toward being overwhelmed.

The way we feel when we experience overwhelming situations is real. However, what was true for Daniel is true for us: the first step in winning the war against worry is understanding that God really is greater than whatever we are going through.

CHAPTER 3

GOD IS BIGGER

My daughter, Charisse, is six years old, and she and I have been doing "Daddy Date Day" every Saturday since she was six months old. Honestly, it was a bit awkward at first, because she didn't have a lot to talk about back then. She didn't care about the weather or sports, and politics didn't capture her attention at all.

When she was a baby, I'd usually get her out of bed and feed her some sort of baby food, and then I'd take her to Chick-fil-A and put her in a high chair, where she'd drool and watch me eat. Recently I realized, though, that she most likely will have the same struggle with me one day if we continue the Daddy Date Day tradition. She will probably take me to Chick-fil-A, put me in a little wheelchair, and I'll sit there and drool while she eats.

As Charisse got older, she was able to help me out a little by telling me what she wanted to do on our dates. On one particular Saturday morning, when she was about two years old, I asked her what she wanted to do that day. Without hesitation she said, "Duck pond."

Here in Anderson, South Carolina, we tend to be pretty simple people. So it's no surprise that everyone refers to the pond with ducks in it as "the duck pond." Charisse had seen families feeding the ducks there, and now she wanted us to buy some bread and do the same.

The thing you must realize about the duck pond is that there are not only ducks but also some geese. I don't know how geese typically behave, but I'm quite convinced that someone must have given these particular geese some crack, because they are the craziest, angriest little animals I've ever seen in my life.

So Charisse and I were feeding the ducks and having a special father-daughter moment, when all of a sudden I heard, "Hisssssss!"

I turned around, and about ten feet away from me was a rather large goose with its neck out and its wings back. It was staring straight at me and seemed to be looking for a fight.

All of a sudden something snapped inside this goose, and it began charging me and making a noise unlike anything I'd ever heard. Now keep in mind that I am six foot six, weigh about 225 pounds, and could have crushed the demon-possessed creature without much effort. However, I completely lost my mind, scooped Charisse into my arms, and began screaming like a girl while running from this stupid goose.

Let's stop for a minute. Can you imagine this scene? A huge dude who's carrying a toddler and running from a goose? Insane.

I was doing an all-out sprint for my life for about ten seconds until I had this thought: *I'm bigger than this!* So I stopped running, turned around with Charisse still in one arm, pointed at the goose with my other arm, and said out loud, "In the name of Jesus, I will punt you!"

I kid you not, the goose stopped dead in its tracks. And yes, I absolutely would have sent this creature on the journey of its life if it had come one step closer.

Later that evening, when I was reflecting on the situation (and feeling thankful that no one was there with a camera phone), I realized, *All too often people who are in Christ run from things that they have power over.*

In Christ we have the authority and the ability to overcome anything the world throws our way—not because of who we are, but rather because of who is in us. The Bible says in 1 John 4:4: "You belong to God, my dear children. You have already won a victory over those people, because the Spirit who lives in you is greater than the spirit who lives in the world."

If we're ever going to experience victory over our overwhelming circumstances, we need to grasp another foundational truth about God's character: He is able. The reality is that God is greater than whatever "goose" is chasing you!

Embracing Your True Identity

Let's go back to our story about Daniel. There are two little words at the beginning of verse eight that have major significance when it comes to understanding how to overcome circumstances. Let's take another look: "*But Daniel* was determined not to defile himself by eating the food and wine given to them by the king. He asked the chief of staff for permission not to eat these unacceptable foods" (Daniel 1:8, emphasis added).

Notice those first two words: "But Daniel." You might rush right past that at first, but here's why it's so meaningful. His captors tried their best to change Daniel's name to a Babylonian name, and in that culture, if you changed someone's name, then you were essentially changing his identity.

The name Daniel means "God is my judge." The Babylonian name Belteshazzar means "Baal saves" or "Baal saves my life." The symbolism here is huge: Daniel never took on the identity of a slave!

We're not reading the book of Belteshazzar but rather the book of Daniel.

The first two words of this verse don't say, "But Belteshazzar"; rather, they say, "But Daniel."

And here's the application for us. If you and I don't want to be overwhelmed by our circumstances, then we can't take on the identity of what used to enslave us. One of the major lessons we need to learn as followers of Jesus is to refuse to identify ourselves by who we used to be or what we happen to be going through now.

In my twenty years in ministry, I've had many conversations with people who tell me, "Perry, I'm an addict."

This is how I always respond: "I hear what you're saying, but let me ask you a question. Are you a Christian—have you surrendered your life to Jesus?"

If they tell me yes, then I am quick to say, "Then you are not an addict! You may be struggling with a particular addiction. It may be claiming victory over you right now. But that doesn't define who you are. However, if you continue to identify yourself by your circumstances rather than by Christ in you, then you will always feel overwhelmed and trapped. And you will always remain a prisoner of your circumstances. It's time to grab hold of the fact that you are not an addict but a child of God!"

> We need to stop identifying ourselves by our slavery and start identifying ourselves with our Savior.

God is bigger than any difficult circumstances we face, any struggles we experience, any mistakes that threaten to define us. We embrace our true identity when we stop identifying ourselves by our slavery and start identifying ourselves with our Savior.

Shedding Your Past

One of the lies many Christians have bought into is the idea that some sins are too big for God to forgive. Some people struggle to move forward in their faith because they can't seem to get beyond their past. I've been preaching about the love and forgiveness Jesus offers for more than two decades, and in that time countless people have approached me after the service to tell me they simply can't believe that Jesus would forgive them for a particular sin that was just too big and too horrible.

When I talk with people who struggle with their past, they often look at what they used to do and allow that to determine who they are. However, the Bible says in 2 Corinthians 5:17, "Anyone who belongs to Christ has become a new person. The old life is gone; a new life has begun!" In other words, we are brand new!

When God saved us, He did far more than merely punch our "get out of hell free" card. The Bible is clear that He also came to live inside us and change us from the inside, and He promises to give us the strength and power to overcome anything we're up against.

He doesn't simply tell us to change; He gives us the power to do so! He's a lot bigger than we give Him credit for.

As long as we identify ourselves by who we used to be, we fall back into that cycle of sin and become overwhelmed with guilt and shame. However, if we step into our new identity as people who have been ransomed by the death of Christ on the cross, and if we embrace the victory He promises us, we are way more likely to overcome whatever is holding us back.

Do your circumstances feel big and overwhelming?

Take heart, because God is bigger.

Are you tempted to define yourself by an old habit or addiction?

God is bigger.

Do the sins of your past loom large in your rearview mirror?

God is bigger.

He's bigger than whatever you're facing—so stop running from the goose and step into who He says you are!

CHAPTER 4

GOD IS ABLE

I absolutely love living in the South. Despite the fact that some people can't seem to get over a war that was fought 150 years ago, it really is a great place to live.

One of the things I find quite fascinating about the South is the number of four-wheel drives that exist here. On top of that, all the drivers of such vehicles seem to be absolutely confident that their trucks can pull anything, climb any hill, and go through any mud hole.

You will find that nearly all these trucks are equipped with a chain saw, a gun rack, and a chain big enough to pull South America and Africa together.

When it snows here, people who have four-wheel drives absolutely lose their minds. Now if you don't live in the Southeastern part of the United States, let me explain. Our road crews in this part of the country are not fully equipped to deal with snow and ice. And hardly anyone around these parts knows how to drive in those conditions.

I often tell people who move here from another part of the country, "If it snows and you get stuck on the side of the road, just stay right there. People in four-wheel drives live for this stuff. They absolutely ignore the news reports that beg people to stay off the roads. They believe their four-wheel drive will be able to overcome the storm, so if you stay put, sooner or later three guys in a truck will come along. And there's no doubt they'll be equipped with food, rescue dogs, a flare gun, and a chain to pull you out of the ditch."

Guys in the South never doubt the power and potential of a truck. They believe it will overcome any situation they happen to get into.

I promise, there's really a connection here. Here goes: so what if followers of Jesus believed in the power of God like rednecks believe in the power of their trucks?

Daniel didn't have a four-wheel-drive camel to get him out of his tough situation; however, he did have an amazing grasp on the power of God, which truly was able to pull him through some overwhelming circumstances.

One of the most fascinating parts about Daniel's story is that God never appears to him at any point and assures him that everything will turn out just fine in the end. God doesn't say, "Okay, Daniel, here's the deal. You're going to have a really bad day soon. All sorts of really awful things are going to happen and you're going to be hit with some crushing circumstances. And here's an even bigger deal. When they offer you food and wine after they take you to Babylon, don't partake of either of them! But if you do all this—if you listen to Me and refuse to drink and eat the stuff of the Babylonians—then I promise I'm going to show up and bless you and make your life as easy as possible. Hey, there's even going to be a book in the Bible named for you. People are going to name their little boys after you, and one day there will even be a VeggieTales episode that talks about what a strong young man you are. Take a stand for Me, and I'll make everything all right."

Daniel didn't have any of those guarantees from God. He just knew that he was in the middle of a situation that was trying to define him and overwhelm him. But he also knew that God was greater than his circumstances and was able to pull him through.

I don't know the details of the overwhelming circumstances you're facing right now. But here's what I know about God: He is greater than anything you're up against, and He's able to pull you through, just as He did for Daniel.

A "Right Now" God

Let's pick up with Daniel's story again: "*Now God* had given the chief of staff both respect and affection for Daniel" (Daniel 1:9, emphasis added).

The most important words in that verse are the first two: "Now God." The reason I want to draw attention to this phrase is because God is a "right now" God! Right now He is at work—no matter what your circumstances, no matter how you're feeling, no matter if you can see Him or not.

Jesus Himself made the same claim about God constantly being at work: "Jesus replied, 'My Father is always working, and so am I'" (John 5:17).

All too often when we get overwhelmed, we start believing that God is merely a "back then" God. We read Bible stories about how God would move in incredible ways and do something amazing, but we decide He either has lost His touch or has merely chosen not to show off like that anymore.

Other times we buy into the idea that He is an "only when" God. We think that maybe He will move and do certain things to rescue us out of the tough spot we're in, but only when we figure out the proper formula. This often leads us to try to be more religious in an effort to get God to see how hard we're trying, thinking He'll be moved by our incredible works of righteousness and eventually decide to rescue us. And then if that doesn't happen, we become discouraged, confused, and even bitter toward God because we think He wasn't pleased with our performance.

But that's not how God operates. He isn't stuck in the past; He doesn't demand that we jump through certain hoops. He's a "right now" God! He's with you right now, working for your good. We're told in Romans 8:28, "We know that God causes everything to work together for the good of those who love God and are called according to his purpose for them."

No Compromise

It sounds good to believe that God is capable and at work behind the scenes, but I should warn you: it won't be easy. Some people won't like it, and they'll actively work against you, trying to convince you otherwise.

When Daniel told the guy in charge of his meals that he wouldn't eat the king's food, here's how the man responded: "I am afraid of my lord the king, who has ordered that you eat this food and wine. If you become pale and thin compared to the other youths your age, I am afraid the king will have me beheaded" (Daniel 1:10).

Anytime you make up your mind that God is able, the world is going to put pressure on you to compromise.

Maybe you're single, and you're hoping and praying that one day you will meet "the one." However, as time passes, the options seem to be getting fewer and fewer. You have high standards for what you're looking for in a mate based on what the Bible teaches; however, people are telling you that you need to be more "realistic" because that person doesn't exist. So you start dating people you know aren't right for you, and you justify it by telling yourself, *Maybe God just needs me to help out a little bit. After all, it is easier to make people godly than it is to make them cute.* And so you begin to drift toward compromise because you believe it would actually be easier to find the lost city of Atlantis than it would be to find someone who really does love Jesus.

Maybe you're married and struggling, really struggling, and you're starting to believe you married the wrong person. You meet someone at work who is so much easier to talk to and seems to understand you better than your spouse does. Eventually you wonder if maybe you need to get out of your current marriage and into a relationship with this other person.

Whatever the specifics of your situation, all of us face the temptation to compromise. What we need to understand is that if we are going to overcome our current circumstances, we will never make it if we flirt with compromise.

Daniel had made up his mind that he wasn't going to budge on this food issue, so he was prepared when the pushback came—even when the guy in charge of him said, "I'm sorry, bro, but this just isn't an option. I'm not going to lose my head over you!" Daniel wasn't merely a follower of God when it was convenient; he also remained faithful when the pressure became intense.

Here's what encourages and challenges me about this story: Daniel knew that God could accomplish more through his conviction than through compromise!

God has never needed anyone to compromise on His commands in order for Him to look better or more attractive to the rest of the world. He doesn't need an image consultant or a makeover. He is able to sustain those who believe His Word and refuse to compromise even in the face of overwhelming circumstances.

Let's take a look at how things worked out for Daniel.

Daniel spoke with the attendant who had been appointed by the chief of staff to look after Daniel, Hananiah, Mishael, and Azariah. "Please test us for ten days on a diet of vegetables and water," Daniel said. "At the end of the ten days, see how we look compared to the other young men who are eating the king's food. Then make your decision in light of what you see." The attendant agreed to Daniel's suggestion and tested them for ten days.

At the end of the ten days, Daniel and his three friends looked healthier and better nourished than the young men who had been eating the food assigned by the king. So after that, the attendant fed them only vegetables instead of the food and wine provided for the others.

God gave these four young men an unusual aptitude for understanding every aspect of literature and wisdom. And God gave Daniel the special ability to interpret the meanings of visions and dreams.

When the training period ordered by the king was completed, the chief of staff brought all the young men to King Nebuchadnezzar. The king talked with them, and no one impressed him as much as Daniel, Hananiah, Mishael, and Azariah. So they entered the royal service. Whenever the king consulted them in any matter requiring wisdom and balanced judgment, he found them ten times more capable than any of the magicians and enchanters in his entire kingdom.

Daniel remained in the royal service until the first year of the reign of King Cyrus.

DANIEL 1:11-21

> **Jesus is not threatened by our circumstances or situation—He is a grave-robbing, water-walking, miracle-working, death-defying God.**

Daniel stood firm on his convictions and refused to compromise—yet God didn't deliver him from his circumstances. Instead, He delivered him *through* his circumstances.

The same God who delivered Daniel can do the same for you. He is not threatened by our circumstances or situation—He is a grave-robbing, water-walking, miracle-working, death-defying God, and He's able to pull you through anything you have to face in this life.

No Cakewalk

While it's true that God is able to do anything, that doesn't mean the life of faith is an easy one. One of the biggest myths in Christianity is that if you love Jesus, do good things, read your Bible, go to church, and follow a host of religious rules, you'll never face overwhelming circumstances or tough times. If you do what's right, your kids will always make good grades, you'll never lose your job, your marriage will always sparkle with excitement and romance, and your dog will never die.

The Bible, however, teaches quite the opposite.

This hit me in the face recently when I was reading the Gospel of John. Jesus' words in chapters 13–16 include some of the most intense lessons Jesus ever taught. At the end of one of the longest teachings of Jesus recorded in Scripture, He said something that completely refutes the idea that overwhelming circumstances never come upon good people: "I have told you all this so that you may have peace in me. Here on earth you will have many trials and sorrows. But take heart, because I have overcome the world" (John 16:33).

The first thing Jesus said is that the purpose of His teachings is to bring us peace. I don't know about you, but I am totally interested in peace! Peace on the inside of me. Peace in my family. Peace in my finances. Peace in my relationships with others. Peace in my relationship with God. And the good news is, that's what Jesus wants for us too.

Now it would have been awesome if Jesus' words had ended right there. However, He went on to say, "Here on earth you will have many trials and sorrows."

Keep in mind as you read this verse that Jesus was talking to His disciples—the people closest to Him on this earth. And He told them that they were going to have trials and sorrows. Not that they *might* have them. Not that He'd offer seven easy steps for them to escape a bad day. But that trials and sorrows were certain to come their way.

If that's what Jesus said to the people who were closest to Him, then why would we ever believe we would escape tough times?

If Jesus had ended things there, I'm quite sure everyone would have been looking for a bus to dive in front of. Instead, He went on to say, "But take heart, because I have overcome the world."

Jesus didn't say, "I will be overwhelmed by the world." He said we could take heart because He has already overcome it!

A couple of years ago I had the privilege of going to Israel for the first time and traveling all over the country. While I was there, I saw the Bible come to life for me in ways I'd never imagined.

I could go on and on about the trip (and the hummus, fish, and fresh olives, which were more delicious than I can describe), but the most powerful experience for me was the time I spent at the Garden Tomb.

At the time, I was fighting an intense battle with depression (which I'll talk about more in chapter 6). I felt like the world had beaten me, spit on me, and whipped me mercilessly, and even worse, I thought God had betrayed me. It was the darkest time of my life, and I wasn't sure if I was ever going to escape it.

Until that day in front of the empty tomb.

I thought about Jesus. My Jesus. I thought about His beaten and bloodied body that had crossed the very threshold I was now standing in front of.

Right there. In that very spot.

The weight of it all felt so heavy on me.

And suddenly I knew that Jesus hadn't just carried the weight of deep sorrow and pain in His body. He'd also carried it in His heart.

He knows what human brokenness feels like.

He knows pain.

He knows *my* pain.

Jesus was betrayed by someone close to Him—someone in His inner circle. I imagine that betrayal cut Him deeper than any whip ever could.

The very people He loved and came to save spit on Him, mocked Him, and beat Him. They stripped Him bare, naked for all the world to see. If anyone understands raw pain, it's my Jesus.

I stood there and let this truth sink deep. Deep into the places of my soul that were desperate for resurrection.

I knew that without Christ, I would constantly be overwhelmed by life. But in Him, I could overcome anything this world might throw my way.

CHAPTER 5

CAN WE BRING OUR MESS TO CHURCH?

Before beginning NewSpring Church in 2000, I served as a youth pastor for a wonderful church for six years. One of my Sunday responsibilities included making the announcements at the beginning of the service.

If you're not familiar with church culture, most churches have a host of activities that take place during the week, and the planners of those activities feel they need to be announced so everyone can make sure to put the event on their calendar.

That meant I was the target of everyone in the church who had an activity they wanted announced. In other words, I could hardly walk to the restroom without having someone say, "Hey, Perry, make sure you announce the Quilting for Jesus meeting this Sunday!" (When I was asked to make that particular announcement, I remember thinking I wasn't completely sure that Jesus ever quilted when He was here on earth. But I usually just did what I was told.)

Announcement time was always a challenge, because not only did I have to make the announcements but I also had to pretend to be excited about them. It was difficult, really, because I was saying things like, "Don't forget the Quilting for Jesus meeting this coming Tuesday night at 7:00," while thinking, *I would not be caught dead at this thing.*

One particular Sunday I was up front getting ready to make the announcements, and right before I walked onto the platform, someone informed me about a woman in our church who was about to have a baby. Apparently her water had broken and she was on her way to the hospital.

At the church I pastor now, it seems like babies are regularly flying out all over the place. However, this other church only had around 150 people, and everyone knew the woman who was about to give birth. Naturally I felt that the entire church should know about it so we could pray for her, her husband, and her child.

So I strolled onto the stage, talked to the church about the various activities coming up that week, and concluded with, "And I was just told something very exciting. Cindy's water broke this morning! [That's not her real name, but we'll go with that.] She's on her way to the hospital to give birth." Everyone in the congregation said, "Ahhhh" in unison, and I felt like I'd done a good job.

Until . . .

After the service, I was approached by a little senior-adult lady who made it a point to come up to me about once a month and tell me something I'd said or done wrong during announcement time. I could tell immediately from the look on her face that she had an agenda that most likely included ripping me to shreds.

She walked right up to me, raised her voice, and said, "We don't talk about that!"

I promise I had no idea what she was talking about. My first thought was, *I know, I thought quilting for Jesus was a bad idea too!* She was angry and I was confused, and before long a small crowd had begun to gather.

"I'm so sorry," I said. "I have obviously offended you. But I have no idea what I said or did. Would you tell me?"

She was more than happy to fulfill my request. "You said that girl's water broke!" she exclaimed.

Before we move on, I feel the need to be completely transparent and admit that at the time, I had no idea what it meant that her water broke. I promise! All I knew was that's what someone had told me and I repeated it, because it obviously had something to do with the birth of a child.

"Is it really a bad thing to say her water broke?"

At this point I think this lady would have taken a swing at me if she'd had a baseball bat on her.

"Yes, it's bad," she said. "In fact, it's awful! It was offensive! You should be ashamed of yourself because *we don't talk about stuff like that in church!*"

At this point a couple of other senior-adult ladies had gathered around her and were looking at me and nodding their heads. I was obviously in hot water. I had done the unthinkable. I suddenly felt the need to ask for forgiveness from the woman who was having the baby.

A couple of days later, I went to the hospital to see Cindy and her new child. Honestly, I wasn't sure how to bring up the subject, so I just came out with it. "Cindy, I owe you a huge apology," I said. "I shared something about you in front of the whole church that I shouldn't have said."

"What did you say?"

"I told them that your water had broken, and I had no idea I wasn't supposed to say something like that." (At that point I still had no idea what that even meant.)

She laughed out loud for a long time. So did her husband. And I felt like the biggest moron on the planet.

"Perry, I promise it's not a big deal," she said. "It happens to nearly every woman who has a baby. No one from the church has said a word to me about it. I'm sure no one is upset."

Afterward I found out what the whole "water breaking" deal actually means, and the more I reflected on why the little old lady had gotten so angry with me, the more I realized what the problem was: if something is messy, then the church isn't supposed to talk about it.

The Problem with Church World

I'm not sure where you happen to live in the world, but I want to be honest here about church culture in the United States. Far too many people attend church not to meet with Jesus but rather to make an appearance.

Originally church began because a dead guy (Jesus) came back to life and His followers just couldn't quit talking about it. There was community. There was celebration.

And perhaps most of all, that's where grace was both received and given.

The reality is that every person we lock eyes with on Sunday morning (including the person we saw in the mirror this morning) needs grace. Before the service even starts, we've all most likely messed something up, lost our temper over a minor issue, or said something we regret. However, when people sit in church pews, the atmosphere isn't usually conducive to people admitting they have a problem and asking for help. Instead, everyone tries to appear as perfect as possible.

Let's get even more real. In many churches in America, a guy can pretty much have sex with as many women as he wants during the week as long as he shows up to church on time the following Sunday with his nicest suit and tie on. Coming to church has nothing to do with who you actually are but rather with how you appear.

A woman can be going down the road of having an affair with an old flame she reconnected with through Facebook, but then she shows up on Sunday with great hair, flawless makeup, and a pair of panty hose, and people think that because of her appearance, everything is great in her life and her walk with the Lord must be stellar.

A couple can have a rebellious child who is absolutely shattering their hearts, but they show up on Sunday and try to hide their pain out of fear that people will discover they aren't the perfect family they've fought so hard to appear to be.

Somehow the perception is that church is for perfect people, for people who have it all together, for people who aren't overwhelmed by their circumstances. Instead of seeing the church as a place to repent of our brokenness and get support in our weakness, we've gotten good at covering up our messes. And even though our lives aren't perfect and things may not be holding together, we've been taught to pretend we're great, to "fake it till we make it."

While this is a cultural understanding of church, it isn't a biblical understanding of what the body of Christ should be.

The book of Acts describes the early church this way: "All the believers devoted themselves to the apostles' teaching, and to fellowship, and to sharing in meals (including the Lord's Supper), and to prayer. . . . All the believers met together in one place and shared everything they had" (Acts 2:42, 44).

It seems the church was put together by God to be more like a family than a group of people fighting to protect their image. And while you can fake it around people who don't really know you, you can't fake it with family!

Every person we lock eyes with (including the person we saw in the mirror this morning) needs grace.

The kind of church culture where people feel they have to pretend their lives are picture-perfect has resulted in two main problems. For one thing, sooner or later a person's "issues" are found out by other people in the church.

This means that either they become the subject of gossip or they are told by church leaders not to come back until the problem is dealt with.

The second problem comes when someone decides they simply can't live with the pressure of appearing to be perfect, so they drop out of church altogether. They know they'll never measure up to the perfection club, so they stop trying.

Somehow church has become a place where we don't want to hear about real issues or relevant struggles or sins we've been dealing with all week long. We'd rather hear obscure history lessons, Greek and Hebrew word training, and lots of quotes from dead white guys.

For example, there are two subjects some church people get upset about every single time I talk about them.

Sex and money!

These are things nearly every adult on the planet thinks about every single day—things we make good and bad decisions about all through our lives. However, when a church addresses these topics, people get angry, because talking about them forces everyone to get real.

I believe that every church in the world is full of messed-up people, and sometimes the prettier they try to be on the outside, the more messed up they really are on the inside.

On the Other Side of the Cross

Take a moment to do an exercise with me. Take a look at the picture below. The people on the left side of the cross represent those who do not know Christ, and the people standing on the right side of the cross represent those who do know Christ.

If you don't know Christ (the left side of the cross), the Bible says you are lost. Your biggest problem isn't that you have struggles or some stuff you are dealing with, but rather that you don't have Jesus in your life. Your biggest need is not to fill your life with more of whatever you're clinging to and may be addicted to; instead, you need a relationship with the God who loves you more than you could ever imagine.

When you meet Christ, you literally cross over from death to life. However, the misconception in church world (by both Christians and non-Christians) is that once we are on the right side of the cross, life becomes easy. People assume that Christians have perfect lives—that we ride unicorns, eat Lucky Charms, and sing happy songs all day long. But I've been doing ministry for more than two decades now, and I can honestly say I've seen just as many people who face hardships on the right side of the cross as on the other side.

When we meet Christ, we are saved from the penalty of sin, but we do not escape the effects of sin—whether that's our own sin or other people's sin or simply the broken world we live in.

When we meet Christ and get on the right side of the cross, our goal isn't to get everyone to think we're perfect and have it all together. Rather, this is where we recognize how much we need Jesus and learn to fall more in love with Him every single day.

When we're feeling overwhelmed—whether as a result of our own sin or simply from living in a fallen world—church is exactly the place we need to go for healing, not the place to hide out in camouflage, pretend we're perfect, or leave because we don't feel we measure up to the people around us.

Jesus didn't surround Himself with perfect people with zero problems. And if He didn't gather perfect people around Him, then why in the world would we expect perfect people to be in a place that is supposed to be His body?

Church shouldn't be the place we run from when we're feeling overwhelmed; it should be the place we run *to*. After all, church is the place where Jesus meets us and changes us into who we need to be.

CHAPTER 6

WINNING THE BATTLE WITH DEPRESSION

I met Christ on May 27, 1990. In all the years since that day, He has been living in me, changing me, and walking with me. But that doesn't mean I'm exempt from some of the messy things in life.

In late 2008, I sank into a black hole that I now know was depression. It was the darkest time of my life, and I honestly wanted to die. I was so desperate to find relief that I seriously thought about ending my own life. And it wasn't because I didn't love Jesus, but rather because I had allowed my life to get out of control.

Believe it or not, people on the right side of the cross struggle with depression.

The sad thing is that in all my years of church work, I can't recall hearing a single message on the subject of depression.[1] I've even heard church leaders say that if a person is dealing with depression, it's because of some unconfessed sin that needs to be dealt with.

The church tends to have trouble talking about depression because it's messy and uncomfortable. But this is something that's not going away. More and more people who show up on Sunday mornings are struggling with this very real issue. I recently saw on a news show that in the past several decades the use of antidepressants has increased

400 percent in North America.[2] We are one of the richest and most depressed countries in the world.

I know there are some people who have trouble with the idea that someone who is truly a follower of Jesus could struggle with depression. If that's the case for you, I would simply encourage you to read your Bible—and not just the uplifting stories but also the parts where it gets so real and raw that we squirm a bit.

Biblical Giants Have Bad Days Too

Case in point: What about Moses? He was one of the godliest men in the Bible, and God used him to lead Israel through some of its most significant moments in history. Moses loved God and listened to Him— in fact, "the LORD would speak to Moses face to face, as one speaks to a friend" (Exodus 33:11). However, Moses went through a time when he just couldn't take it anymore. Moses reached his breaking point and said to God, "I can't carry all these people by myself! The load is far too heavy! If this is how you intend to treat me, just go ahead and kill me. Do me a favor and spare me this misery!" (Numbers 11:14-15).

> Even godly people who really love Jesus can and do deal with depression.

Wow, did you catch that? One of the godliest men in the Bible asked God to kill him? It sounds to me like he was a little depressed—maybe even suicidal.

Then there's Elijah, one of the most powerful prophets in the Bible. In 1 Kings 18 we read that he went on top of Mount Carmel and called down fire from heaven in the midst of a contest against a false god. (I'm going to go out on a limb here and say that none of us have ever seen that kind of success.) Yet after this major victory, we see him at the end of his rope when he was threatened by the queen.

> Elijah was afraid and fled for his life. He went to Beersheba, a town in Judah, and he left his servant there. Then he went on

alone into the wilderness, traveling all day. He sat down under a solitary broom tree and prayed that he might die. "I have had enough, LORD," he said. "Take my life, for I am no better than my ancestors who have already died."

1 KINGS 19:3-4

Wow, have you ever been there? "I have had enough, LORD. . . . Take my life." If Elijah, a biblical hero, experienced such a low point, why are we surprised when we're hit by such feelings ourselves?

Let's talk about one more person—the apostle Paul. If anyone loved Jesus and lived for Him, it was Paul. And yet we read these words in his letter to the Corinthian church: "We think you ought to know, dear brothers and sisters, about the trouble we went through in the province of Asia. We were crushed and overwhelmed beyond our ability to endure, and we thought we would never live through it" (2 Corinthians 1:8).

Scripture says that Paul and his traveling companion, Timothy, were so overwhelmed that they didn't think they were going to make it.

What these examples from Scripture make clear is that godly people who really love Jesus can and do deal with depression.

When a Bad Day Gets Even Worse

The truth is that depression isn't just sparked by a bad mood or a lack of faith. Sometimes it comes as a result of circumstances that are out of our control or people with an evil agenda.

That's precisely the kind of situation Daniel found himself in. We pick up his story again with a look at the king of Babylon during the time of Daniel's capture. Babylon had a string of power-hungry kings, but Nebuchadnezzar might have been one of the most unstable rulers of them all.

In order to get a clear picture of Nebuchadnezzar, there are some things we need to understand about that culture and time period. If the people didn't like the guy in power, there wasn't a process to vote him out. Instead, a group of people would get together and try to kill him. As a result, kings tended to be somewhat insecure individuals.

One of the cultural beliefs at the time was that dreams were important messages from the gods. Therefore, kings had people on their staff who specialized in the interpretation of dreams.

In Daniel 2, we read that Nebuchadnezzar had a dream that absolutely freaked him out. So he woke up, called in his entourage of wise men and astrologers, and desperately tried to figure out what the dream meant.

Typically in this situation, the king would tell his group of men about the dream, and in turn they would tell him what it meant. But in this case, Nebuchadnezzar was apparently having some trust issues with his inner circle of wise men, so he shook things up a bit.

> One night during the second year of his reign, Nebuchadnezzar had such disturbing dreams that he couldn't sleep. He called in his magicians, enchanters, sorcerers, and astrologers, and he demanded that they tell him what he had dreamed. As they stood before the king, he said, "I have had a dream that deeply troubles me, and I must know what it means."
>
> Then the astrologers answered the king in Aramaic, "Long live the king! Tell us the dream, and we will tell you what it means."
>
> But the king said to the astrologers, "I am serious about this. If you don't tell me what my dream was and what it means, you will be torn limb from limb, and your houses will be turned into heaps of rubble! But if you tell me what I dreamed and what the dream means, I will give you many wonderful gifts and honors. Just tell me the dream and what it means!"
>
> DANIEL 2:1-6

Essentially the king was telling these men, "First of all, you need to tell me what I dreamed, and then you need to tell me what it means.

If you can do this, I will reward you handsomely. But if you can't, I'm killing all of you!"

Uh, anyone see a problem here? The wise men apparently did, because they offered a little pushback to his insane idea. "They said again, 'Please, Your Majesty. Tell us the dream, and we will tell you what it means'" (Daniel 2:7).

Nutty Nebuchadnezzar, however, stood by his idea. Here was his response: "I know what you are doing! You're stalling for time because you know I am serious when I say, 'If you don't tell me the dream, you are doomed.' So you have conspired to tell me lies, hoping I will change my mind. But tell me the dream, and then I'll know that you can tell me what it means" (Daniel 2:8-9).

The wise men were feeling some intense pressure at this point. They knew something had to give, so they tried to reason with the king by saying, "No one on earth can tell the king his dream! And no king, however great and powerful, has ever asked such a thing of any magician, enchanter, or astrologer! The king's demand is impossible. No one except the gods can tell you your dream, and they do not live here among people" (Daniel 2:10-11).

That's about the point when Nebuchadnezzar completely lost his mind. "The king was furious when he heard this, and he ordered that all the wise men of Babylon be executed. And because of the king's decree, men were sent to find and kill Daniel and his friends" (Daniel 2:12-13).

Now if you're Daniel, this has to be a little frustrating. You just stood firm on your convictions about what to eat and drink, and the Lord spared your life. Then all of a sudden, a group of guys you weren't even with made the king really mad and now you're going to be killed for it.

Can you imagine the conversation? Daniel is sitting in his house playing Angry Birds on his iPhone, and out of nowhere comes a knock at the door. He goes to open it, and it's someone he recognizes from the castle.

"Hi, Daniel. I'm here to kill you," the guy says.

There's just no way to put a positive spin on this. Through no fault of his own, Daniel found himself right in the middle of some very over-whelming circumstances.

We may not have faced a crazy king, but all of us have been there. Some of us are there right now.

In that moment of intense pressure, Daniel didn't freak out or lose his mind or lose hope. Instead, he responded in a way that serves as an example of how we can respond when overwhelming situations hit us out of nowhere.

CHAPTER 7

MY STORY

I was born in 1971 in Whittier, California, into a non-Christian home. My mom and dad were good, hardworking people; however, when people don't know Christ, the potential for sin in their lives is pretty much unlimited. Without sharing too much, I'll just sum it up by saying that I wasn't born into the most stable home environment.

When I was around two or three years old, my mom visited a church, and after the service, she told the pastor she'd like him to come to our house. She informed my dad of the pastor's visit at the last minute, just before he arrived. My dad cussed her out and then promptly hid the beer he was drinking.

The pastor and one of the deacons shared the gospel with my parents that night, and both of them prayed to receive Christ. They were baptized and joined the church the following Sunday, where they attended faithfully until my family moved to upstate South Carolina when I was around four years old.

I lived in a little town called Easley from the time I was five until I went to college at nineteen. Honestly, I thought my life and my family were pretty normal . . . until I went to counseling as an adult and began to discover how dysfunctional things really were.

From the time I was five until I was about eleven or twelve, a few things happened to me that I put off and refused to deal with for many years. I was molested by two different people in that time period. I never told anyone about it until I was in college because I felt gross and like I'd done something to cause it.

When I was in fifth grade, my mother and father separated and nearly got divorced when it came to light that my dad was having an affair. Believe it or not, during that time I began to develop some massive authority issues, anger issues, and trust issues. I didn't know Christ then, so I turned to food for my comfort.

Eventually my parents were able to work through the infidelity. My mother forgave my dad, and they reconciled the marriage. However, less than a year later, when I was twelve years old, my mother discovered she had cancer. She went to be with Jesus three months later.

Can anyone say *bitterness*? I was already mad at my dad. I absolutely loved my mom, and now God had "taken her home." (At least that's what people at the church kept telling me.) I was angry at God for taking my mom. Really angry.

All my life I had believed that God was great, that He was good, and that He answered prayers. But at that point, I decided all three of those statements were lies.

After mom died, things got really weird in my house. As I look back now, I believe my dad was either bipolar or dealing with depression, but at any rate, he didn't know how to process everything that had happened. It was during this time that my dad became emotionally and verbally abusive to me. When I got home from school, I didn't know if I was going to get a hug or get cussed out. Over the next seven years he married and divorced twice, and it was, to say the least, a crazy environment to grow up in.

During my teen years, I went from being addicted to just food to being addicted to food and porn. And I spent the next several years accumulating a lot of baggage.

When I was in high school, a guy I knew was pretty relentless in inviting me to church. Eventually I caved and started going with him because he promised there were "hot girls" there.

After attending for several months, I surrendered my life to Christ. On that day I moved from the left side of the cross to the right side of the cross—all because of God's grace in my life. However, I still had baggage I was carrying from the other side that I simply refused to deal with.

It wasn't long before I became incredibly self-righteous and legalistic in my young faith. I developed a works-based theology, and I went all out trying to prove myself. Of all the words people would have used to describe me during my college years, I can assure you that none would have been *lazy*. My counselor told me that I did this as a defense mechanism so I'd never have to go back to the unstable home I'd grown up in. I worked as hard as I could to put myself through college and managed to finish in four years. During my senior year, I actually worked three jobs to make ends meet. I was constantly striving to prove myself, to be good enough.

I met my wife, Lucretia, in 1996 and we got married in 2000—the same year we started NewSpring Church. Lucretia had just finished medical school and was going into a three-year family practice residency program, which basically meant she was expected to work all the time. And since we'd just started a church, I did nothing but work during that time as well. I'd spend anywhere between sixty and eighty hours a week neck deep in church stuff, often operating on four to five hours of sleep.

The pace I was setting for my life was simply unsustainable.

NewSpring began with around fifteen people who met in a living room. We held our first service on January 16, 2000, with 115 people in attendance. Within six months we'd grown to two services, and a year after that, we had to move facilities because we'd expanded so much. In 2002 we went from averaging about 500 people a week to around 1,600 people—all in a matter of six weeks. The next year we broke the 2,000 barrier and then the 3,000 barrier within the span of a few months. Each year we were adding services, adding staff, and adding responsibility, and I was depending on adrenaline like a crack addict counts on his next hit.

Then in 2005, I nearly died.

And I'm not just trying to be overdramatic here. I had minor surgery that year that resulted in some major complications, and I spent several days on my back in ICU. Looking back, I believe that the Lord was using this situation to try to get my attention. But there were schedules to keep, meetings to lead, and problems to solve, so I jumped back into the fray as soon as I could.

In 2006 our church moved into a brand-new facility, and within seven months, our attendance went from 4,000 people to 8,000 people. More staff, more responsibility; less rest, less time for fun—and somehow I managed to justify it all.

In 2007 Lucretia and I had our daughter, Charisse. (Mainly Lucretia had her—I was there for moral support!) My attitude was that I would love my little baby girl, but her arrival into our home wasn't going to affect my schedule. No way—I couldn't slow down. I was Superman; I had to rescue the world. So right after Charisse's birth, our church began a capital campaign in which we were attempting to raise millions of dollars for the expansion of our ministry. That meant I was working seventy-plus hours a week with a newborn at home and getting no sleep.

As our attendance increased and awareness about our church spread, it became obvious that some people who called themselves Christians didn't like what we were doing or how we were doing it. As a result, a flurry of criticism and personal attacks came my way. This was something I'd never experienced before, and it took an intense emotional toll.

I remember going on a date with Lucretia in December of that year. We were sitting at Outback, and I simply couldn't take it anymore. I told her, "We have a great house, we have nice cars, we're living comfortably, and the church is growing at a rate I never thought it would. I'm getting asked to travel and speak at conferences all over the country. *And I hate my life!*"

Over the next three years, I experienced days that were so dark, so difficult, and so overwhelming that I considered taking my own life. I finally decided not to do it after I concluded that it would be the most selfish, cowardly act I could commit, and the pain I would cause my wife, my little girl, and my close friends wouldn't be worth it. But I still remember some of those long days when I just wanted out of here.

• • •

That's my story . . . and I know you have one as well. Maybe life was great until you had a job transfer and now you are dealing with more than you can handle. Maybe your first child was an angel but your second one seems to be a little devil, and you feel like you're falling apart as a parent. Maybe your aging parents took a turn for the worse and at some point you realized that you are now responsible for their future.

Many times depression isn't the result of one massive tragic event that unfolds in our lives. Rather, it's the accumulation of many seemingly small things that aren't dealt with and continue building on one another.

Maybe you're there too, and you just want out. Maybe you feel like God is a million miles away and has completely given up on you.

If that's you right now, let me share some good news: you don't have to stay there. There is light at the end of your tunnel—there's a way out. But the way out isn't a quick fix, like praying a little prayer or increasing your spiritual activity. The reality is that if you're overwhelmed to the point of wanting to walk away from everything or even end it all, you didn't get there overnight. And it's going to take time to get out of this place too.

> **Often depression isn't the result of one massive tragic event. Rather, it's the accumulation of many seemingly small things that build on one another.**

Are you willing to do whatever it takes to get out of the mess you're in? As I've learned from my personal struggle, God is faithful and will do His part, but we must be faithful to do ours.

CHAPTER 8

WARNING SIGNS THAT YOU'RE HEADING FOR A CRASH

I *love* speed (going fast—not the drug!). So you can imagine my excitement when I borrowed a friend's sports car one time. It had 500 horsepower, and at one point I got it up to ninety in our church parking lot. I can distinctly remember the RPM meter nearly pegging out. Needless to say, I had it in the red.

I know enough about cars to know that you can't keep it in the red for long before the engine completely breaks down. The same applies to our lives. If we go through life at Mach 2 with our hair on fire, eventually we'll hit a wall, and it won't be pretty.

If you're racing through life like I was a few years ago, here are four warning signs that you're on a collision course.

Sign #1: An Unrealistic Pace

No matter what our job or life phase, it's hard to avoid being busy in our society.

We all have things that keep us sprinting from one thing to the next. I once heard someone say, "If I were the devil, I would invent a device you could hold in your hands that would ensure you'd always have your schedule in front of you and give people access to you anytime they wanted."

Ouch!

Several years ago I was in Wyoming on a snowmobile trip. And yes, I was trying to see how fast I could make that thing go—I think I was actually able to hit 70 mph a time or two. I remember on one particular straightaway I was absolutely flying, but then something happened to one of the group members that forced us to wait for a minute or two. I wasn't happy about stopping, but as I sat there, I began to look around and see the mountains and the trees. Honestly, it was one of the most breathtaking scenes I've ever witnessed. In that moment my counselor's words came flooding into my mind: "It's only when we slow down and see the beauty that we can experience intimacy."

There are many people—good people, Christian people—who have zero intimacy in their relationship with God because they don't take the time to see His beauty. We're always in a hurry, always pressing the schedule, always saying, "Hurry up," and we miss all the ways He reveals Himself to us.

> **The Bible calls those who will not work lazy, but it calls those who will not rest disobedient.**

During my busy ministry season, I set a pace that was absolutely unsustainable. One night I was giving my daughter a bath, and as I was getting her out of the bathtub, she was a bit distracted by all the toys around her. "Charisse, come on," I told her. "We've got to hurry."

She stopped me in my tracks when she asked, "Why, Daddy? Where do we have to be?"

I had no answers. I had allowed myself to adopt a breakneck pace, and I was teaching my daughter to do the same thing.

A godly friend confronted me about this when I was searching for a way out of my darkness. "Your pace is unsustainable," he told me. "You are going way too fast."

Depressed people often become angry with those who point out the obvious places they need to make adjustments. Honestly, I didn't want to make adjustments. I didn't want to change. I thought everyone else around me needed to change. I needed a pill. I needed a prayer. I needed someone to understand.

I remember telling my friend, "The devil never takes a day off!"

"Perry," he replied, "I'm not sure the devil is supposed to be your example!"

During those busy years, I hated to hear the word *rest*. I didn't even want to talk about it, although I had trouble avoiding the topic when I studied Scripture—specifically the Ten Commandments. It was hard to get past the fact that the one commandment God spent the most time explaining was the one on rest.

Finally my counselor told me, "The Bible calls those who will not work lazy, but it calls those who will not rest disobedient."

Almost all of us have too many things to do in a given day—go to meetings, get the kids to practice, prepare meals, and check our phones twenty times per hour. However, along the way I've learned the importance of saying no sometimes.

We'll never escape the black hole of being busy if we allow everyone else's demands to determine our schedules.

Sign #2: Unrealistic Expectations of Others

Worried and depressed people tend to be mad at other people.

If you are going through a season of depression right now, odds are you're mad at someone—heck, you may even be mad at *me* by this point.

The reason we get mad is because it's easier to assume that it's someone else's fault than to accept that there's a deeper problem going on.

I did more damage to my marriage during my three-year battle with depression than I ever thought I was capable of. Why? Because I blamed Lucretia for everything. I thought if she would just give me more encouragement, more affection, more attention, my life would be okay. How would you like to be the spouse on the other end of that?

When we took our marriage vows, we both said, "For better, for worse." For three years I showed her what "for worse" was. When I came out of my depression, I repented of my sin, apologized to her, and thanked her for sticking by me. She encouraged me and supported me, and I promised her I would spend the rest of my life showing her what the "for better" part of our vows looked like.

When we are walking through depression, we usually wait on everyone around us to change. And like it or not, that's not going to happen. If you are depressed and blaming those around you, it is time to stop. To blame is to "b-lame"! It's not the fault of your coworkers, your spouse, your kids, the person you're dating, your in-laws, or your dog. The fact is that every single person in your life could change and it wouldn't change your situation, because you've simply developed unrealistic expectations of them.

If you're going through a season of blaming others and believing that your problems will be solved if they change, you are headed down a path that will not lead to a good destination.

I finally came to the point where I asked the Lord to change me and my attitude rather than asking Him to change all the people around me.

Recognizing the role we play in a situation isn't easy, because we live in a society that encourages us to blame everyone else for our problems. People who have a victim mentality—those who constantly tend to blame others—never walk in the victory Jesus promises.

It's easy to point our fingers at the changes other people need to make. But I came to realize that I needed to stop pointing fingers and begin looking in the mirror!

Sign #3: An Unrealistic View on Life

I was angry and upset, and I couldn't sleep. But I was also exhausted, which didn't make sense. Why couldn't I sleep if I was so tired?

Have you ever been there?

You're wide awake in the middle of the night and you know you're tired, but the more you lie there, unable to sleep, the more frustrated you become.

Lucretia told me during that time that I was an emotional roller coaster, a modern-day Dr. Jekyll and Mr. Hyde. And anytime someone would confront me about this, my go-to excuse was, "This is just a phase of life I'm going through. I'll get over it."

The problem was that my anxiety and depression weren't things I needed to get over but things I needed to walk through . . . and that walk is a tough one. If there had been a quick fix or a simple formula that could have pulled me out of my problems, I never would have realized what had gotten me to a place of hopelessness in the first place. I would have continued down a path of insanity, thinking I would somehow attain different results by doing the same things over and over. The path toward healing took time, but ultimately it was worth it.

Sign #4: An Unrealistic Desire to Be Liked by Everyone

I hate to be hated.

And there was a time in my life when it ripped my heart out to know that some people in the world didn't like me.

Let's get something out there right now: not everyone on this planet is going to like you. It doesn't matter what you do, what your hairstyle looks like, what type of music you listen to, or how nice you are. Someone somewhere is going to hate you. And thinking you can do anything to change other people's minds will lead you to insanity.

The Bible says that in Jesus' day, some people believed in Him but were afraid to admit it because they cared so much what other people thought of them. "They loved human praise more than the praise of God" (John 12:43). We need to make sure we are seeking God's approval, not the approval of people we may not even recall ten years from now.

Getting Off the Collision Course

If you are overwhelmed and heading for a crash right now, it's probably because of a combination of two things.

The first is what has happened to you. I'm the last one who will try to sugarcoat anyone's tragic circumstances. What happened to you is legit. You were wounded in some way, and the baggage you carry is heavy.

Maybe you were abused or raped or abandoned. And the message in this book is not "get over it," because the load that's weighing you down is real. But you will need to look at your past and deal with the things that have wounded you.

You can never move forward until you deal with the things you carry with you.

Second, you may be stuck on a crash course because of the choices you've made. We all have to admit that we are where we are, at least in part, because of the choices we've made along the way. If you want to overcome your overwhelming circumstances, you're going to have to look hard at the choices you make. Period. You're going to have to stop identifying yourself as a victim. You're going to have to stop blaming other people. You're going to have to own your life, your decisions.

In the next chapter, we'll talk about ways you can escape what you're trapped in. Daniel escaped! I escaped! And I believe that you can escape as well.

CHAPTER 9

SHATTERING THE CHAINS THAT HOLD YOU BACK

Several years ago I drove to the Hartsfield-Jackson Airport with a friend of mine. We spent some time in Atlanta traffic and were running late. (If you've ever had the pleasure of experiencing this Atlanta phenomenon, then you totally understand what I'm talking about.)

As I was fracturing the speed limit in an all-out attempt to make our flight, we turned off the exit ramp to take us to the airport. All of a sudden I heard a *pop!* followed by *bump, bump, bump.*

I'm sure you know immediately what was happening. I had a flat tire. I knew it, my friend knew it, and the people behind me who were being hit with the rubber from my tire knew it.

But I just kept driving at seventy-five miles per hour, with no intention of slowing down, all the while fighting to keep the car on the road.

Finally my friend said, "Uh, so, are we really going to just keep doing this?"

"What are you talking about?" I asked.

"I really think you have a flat tire."

"Roll down the window and see if either of the tires on your side are flat," I commanded.

He rolled down the window, and rubber from the right front tire flew in his face. I think he may have actually suffered two black eyes. He managed to get his head back inside the car and said, "Uh, yep, the right front tire is shredded. I think I actually saw sparks flying."

I didn't slow down. Seriously, I thought, *If I just keep pushing through, I think we can make it.*

We didn't make it! And it was an awful mess to get things fixed.

I tried to deny the problem, and in doing so, I put the life of my friend in jeopardy as well as my own life.

Denial Doesn't Help; It Only Hurts

The point is this: we can't deny what we're going through and expect things to get better on their own.

If you're trying to deny that you're dealing with some sort of depression or feeling overwhelmed with your life, you're no wiser than I was on the way to the airport that day. And like it or not, you aren't the only person being affected. It's also impacting your friends, your family, and those you work with and interact with every day.

Let's take another look at Daniel's story. I love the fact that Daniel didn't try to deny that there was a problem. He didn't say, "Well, I'm sure the king won't try to kill *me*—I wasn't even there, for crying out loud." His response to the situation demonstrates his willingness to tackle the problem head on.

> When Arioch, the commander of the king's guard, came
> to kill them, Daniel handled the situation with wisdom
> and discretion. He asked Arioch, "Why has the king issued
> such a harsh decree?" So Arioch told him all that had
> happened. Daniel went at once to see the king and requested
> more time to tell the king what the dream meant.
> DANIEL 2:14-16

It's pretty safe to say that this wasn't the kind of news Daniel wanted to hear that day. I'm pretty sure he didn't have "Figure out how to convince the king not to kill me and my friends" anywhere on his to-do list.

In the face of that unforeseeable circumstance, Daniel had a choice: he could deny the problem, or he could deal with it head on.

If Daniel had chosen to pretend that the king didn't really intend to kill him and his friends, he certainly would have lost his life. But by choosing to deal with the problem directly, he was able to escape a life-threatening situation.

If you want to overcome your circumstances, you can't run away from them. You have to address them. And addressing them means admitting you have a problem.

There's one thing that keeps most people from admitting their problems—the same thing that kept me from admitting I was depressed for more than two years. Yep, it's good old-fashioned pride. Pride leads to one inevitable place: imprisonment. And you know what we find in prison? Emotional death, spiritual death, relational death . . . and in some cases, even physical death.

The first step to freedom is to face whatever we're up against.

We Can't Do Life Alone

What happens next in Daniel's story is pretty amazing to me.

Daniel was one of the strongest, godliest men in the Bible, one of the major prophets, one of the guys we name our children after today. Yet when this Bible hero discovered he was in the middle of overwhelming circumstances, he didn't try to go it alone. Instead, he went straight to his friends.

> Then Daniel went home and told his friends Hananiah, Mishael, and Azariah what had happened. He urged them to ask the God of heaven to show them his mercy by telling them the secret, so they would not be executed along with the other wise men of Babylon. That night the secret was revealed to Daniel in a vision. Then Daniel praised the God of heaven.
> DANIEL 2:17-19

One of the strongest men in Scripture knew he couldn't do life alone, so he went to his friends and said, "Guys, I'm in an overwhelming situation. My life is at stake. Oh, and by the way, your lives are at stake as well." His friends didn't judge him, they didn't criticize him, they didn't gossip about him and disguise it as prayer, and they didn't ask him to leave. Instead, they rallied around him, and together, through the power of God, they overcame their problem.

We all need one another.

Men should have other men in their lives who do more than talk football and lie about how good they used to be at sports in high school.

Women should have other godly women in their lives whose goal when they get together isn't to outdo one another in fashion or the performance of their children.

We weren't made to do life alone. Daniel knew he couldn't. Even Jesus didn't do life alone. When He went to the garden of Gethsemane the night before He was crucified, He took Peter, James, and John with Him.

> **The church needs to be a place where it's okay not to be okay.**

That's why I am big on the church not being a place where the perception is perfection, but rather a place where it's okay not to be okay. Now, it's not okay to stay not okay, but I believe that church should be a place where people can admit they're struggling with issues in their lives without fear of being thrown out or becoming the focus of the rumor mill.

I have to admit I was a little scared about how my friends would react when I finally admitted I was depressed and needed counseling. And I didn't fear them because of anything they'd said or done in the past; it was my own pride and insecurity. When I finally admitted my problem, however, they rallied around me, supported me, and stood by me.

I believe I came out of my period of depression a lot more quickly than I would have otherwise because I had a supportive wife and great friends who stood by me and walked every step with me.

So whatever is tearing you up inside, stop hiding it. The sooner you ask for help and admit you need other people, the sooner you will find relief.

Addressing What's Broken on the Inside

In the midst of my depression, I was willing to do just about anything to find relief. It took me a long time, but finally I understood that my relief would only come through repentance.

I wanted God to pull me out of the situation, but His desire was to lead me through it.

We can experience a major shift in our perspective when instead of asking God to pull us out of something, we ask Him to lead us through it. Everything changed when I stopped praying, "Change my friends, change my circumstances, change my wife," and I began to pray, "God, change me, change my heart. Something is wrong with me—please do a work in me!"

> I wanted God to pull me out of the situation, but His desire was to lead me through it.

And do you know what? He did!

This might not be what you want to hear right now, but if you find yourself in a situation similar to mine, it may be time to humble yourself before God and ask, "What's broken inside of me?"

When I finally began to understand that the problem was what was wrong inside of me, the Lord began to show me I had pride issues, anger issues, and fear-of-man issues. And through His mercy, He enabled me to make adjustments that eventually led me out of that dark hole known as depression.

What did God do for Daniel in his dark hole? Quite simply, He gave Daniel a greater view of Himself, which is the greatest thing He can do for any of us. This is what Daniel said about God:

Praise the name of God forever and ever,
for he has all wisdom and power.

He controls the course of world events;
> he removes kings and sets up other kings.

He gives wisdom to the wise
> and knowledge to the scholars.

He reveals deep and mysterious things
> and knows what lies hidden in darkness,
> though he is surrounded by light.

I thank and praise you, God of my ancestors,
> for you have given me wisdom and strength.

You have told me what we asked of you
> and revealed to us what the king demanded.

DANIEL 2:20-23

I can honestly say that my walk with Jesus is closer today than it has ever been—not because He delivered me out of my circumstances, but because He delivered me through them. Jesus not only saved me from hell, but He saved me from *me*.

If God can bring Daniel through the trials he experienced, and if God can bring me through the three painful years of depression I went through, then God can bring you through whatever you're experiencing too. I don't care if you've been in your situation for three months or thirty years, the Bible says that "Jesus Christ is the same yesterday, today, and forever" (Hebrews 13:8).

In other words, if He did it then, He can do it again!

Experiencing a Breakthrough

Daniel went before Nebuchadnezzar and did everything the king asked—he not only told him his dream but also gave the interpretation of the dream. Scripture says that Nebuchadnezzar absolutely lost his mind—in a good way—at that point.

> King Nebuchadnezzar threw himself down before Daniel
> and worshiped him, and he commanded his people to offer

sacrifices and burn sweet incense before him. The king said to Daniel, "Truly, your God is the greatest of gods, the Lord over kings, a revealer of mysteries, for you have been able to reveal this secret."

Then the king appointed Daniel to a high position and gave him many valuable gifts. He made Daniel ruler over the whole province of Babylon, as well as chief over all his wise men. At Daniel's request, the king appointed Shadrach, Meshach, and Abednego to be in charge of all the affairs of the province of Babylon, while Daniel remained in the king's court.

DANIEL 2:46-49

God prospered Daniel after one of the most overwhelming circumstances he had ever gone through. If you are going through overwhelming circumstances—if you feel like life is about to crush you—then maybe, just maybe, God isn't punishing you but is actually preparing to prosper you, just like He did for Daniel.

Only God can use our pain for progress.

My prayer for you is that no matter what you're going through, you will experience hope. God can and will walk with you through this, but you must have the courage to admit you have a problem, accept help, and then ask God to reveal what's broken inside of you.

I need to be honest with you as I conclude this chapter. The battle over depression still rages in me at times. The enemy hits me with it more often than I care to admit. But I know that if the Lord brought me to this, then He will see me through it.

God delivered Daniel.

God delivered me.

He wants to deliver you.

CHAPTER 10

OVERCOMING STRESS AND ANXIETY

It was very late on a Saturday night. Lucretia and I had finally put Charisse to bed, taken care of a few things for the night, and gotten into bed. I had just begun to doze off when it happened.

Chirp!

I knew what it was, but I tried to deny it. I just lay there pretending it wasn't happening.

Then I heard it again.

Chirp!

You've probably figured it out by this point. Sure enough, a battery in one of our smoke detectors was letting me know at this inconvenient point in the night that it needed to be replaced.

So I did what most people who call themselves Christians do when faced with a situation like this. I asked Jesus to make it stop! (He can do anything, right?)

Chirp!

At this point I started getting stressed. Physically stressed, because I was going to have to get up and figure out which stupid smoke detector was freaking out. Emotionally stressed, because I had to preach the next day and this was cutting into my sleep. And spiritually stressed, because despite my prayer, God didn't just make it all better.

Chirp!

Lucretia and I finally got out of bed at the same time. Then we began the tedious process of figuring out which battery needed to be replaced. I'm not sure if you've ever done this before, but basically you have to go stand under each smoke detector until you hear the noise and figure out if the one you're standing under is "the one."

Chirp!

After several stressful minutes of this, I was angry. (It's a fact of life: when you get stressed, you get angry.) I was supposed to be in bed in a state of blissful sleep, but instead I was walking around my house in my underwear looking for a demon-possessed smoke detector.

I was mad at my circumstances. I was mad at my batteries. I was mad at my wife (after all, she should have found the battery by now). And when you become angry, you begin having irrational thoughts. I honestly began entertaining the idea of ripping all the smoke detectors out of the ceiling! (That's not a joke!)

Chirp!

We walked around the house for thirty minutes and waited under every smoke detector, but we still couldn't find the one that was losing its mind. And then we made an amazing discovery: it wasn't one of the smoke detectors that was making the noise; it was the carbon monoxide detector.

By this point I had broken out into a sweat and was ready to start throwing things. I took the carbon monoxide detector out of the wall, ripped out the batteries, and put it on our coffee table, where I planned to deal with it the next day.

No more chirping! I went back to bed, assuming everything was fine now. Right?

Wrong!

When you get stressed, not only do you become angry but you also tend to experience anxiety in the form of extremely irrational thoughts. As I tried to go to sleep, my mind was invaded with thoughts like these:

What if there is really carbon monoxide in our house and it wasn't the batteries but the actual alarm?

What if my family is about to die?

What if my house really is on fire?

What if there's a fire in the basement? It could be—after all, we didn't check down there.

After about three minutes of stress-induced irrational thinking, I had everyone in our home dead and buried in my mind.

Stress and anxiety most often come our way when we experience things that are unplanned or that we are unprepared for.

We experience stress when the professor walks into the classroom and says, "I hope everyone is ready for this test, because it will count as half of your grade," and we forgot to study.

We experience stress when we get the bill in the mail that we weren't expecting.

We experience stress when the doctor calls and wants to speak with us about something that doesn't look normal.

We experience stress when the school calls and tells us they have some concerns about our child.

These things bring legitimate stress into our lives. The point of this chapter is not to show you how to get rid of stressful situations. As long as we live on this big ball of dirt called Earth, we're going to go through things that cause stress. There will never be a time in your life when you don't have some kind of stressful situation coming your way.

> As long as we live on this big ball of dirt called Earth, we're going to go through things that cause stress.

And if you can't think of any reason to feel stressed at the moment, just turn on any twenty-four-hour news network, and within thirty minutes, you'll want to build a bomb shelter in your basement and stock up on food and ammo.

Anxiety-causing situations are here to stay until Jesus comes back.

So instead of seeking how to get out of our stressful situations, we should seek how we can walk through them well. I'm going to share two foundational beliefs that have been extremely helpful to me in my own battles with stress and anxiety. These beliefs are essential for anyone who wants to stop feeling overwhelmed, no matter what their specific circumstances are.

Believe That God Is Holy and Good

All of us change—physically, emotionally, and spiritually. We change our minds about things. Our personalities change, our perspectives change, our relationships change. However, God never changes.

The first thing we need to grasp about His unchanging character is that He is holy. In fact, the word *holy* is the only word in the Bible that's used three consecutive times to describe the character of God. No one ever sees Him and says, "Grace, grace, grace" or "Love, love, love," but on several occasions the angels say, "Holy, holy, holy" (Isaiah 6:3; Revelation 4:8).

Holy means perfect.

Holy means without sin.

And holy is who God is.

God's holiness means He has never made a mistake. He has never had to say, "Oops," "My bad," or "I'm so sorry—I really messed that up." His track record is flawless when it comes to getting things right.

God is not only holy, He is also good. The Bible is full of verses about the Lord's goodness. The psalms in particular tell about how His goodness is ingrained as part of His character: "Give thanks to the Lord, for he is good!" (Psalm 136:1).

From time to time I meet people who ask if there's anything God can't do. My answer is always the same: "He can't stop being holy, and He can't stop being good."

Holiness and goodness are not what He does but rather who He is. And He can't cease to be who He is.

But here's the pushback to this idea: "If God is holy and good, then why do so many bad things happen?"

At this point you may be expecting me to lecture you for thinking such an ungodly thought; however, I'm actually going to congratulate you for asking that question, because it's nothing more than an open door to discover who God is.

I know this well because I asked this question when my mother died of cancer when I was twelve years old. I asked God to heal her, but He didn't. And I had a lot of questions.

I struggled with this again a couple of years ago when my father was suffering with Alzheimer's disease. It was so hard to walk into the nursing home to visit him and have him not even know my name. I remember getting in my car afterward and saying, "Okay, God, I know the Bible says You are good, but why do I have to watch my dad suffer like this?"

As I thought back on all the times in my life when I'd doubted God's holiness and goodness, I realized that the reason for my doubts was because He didn't do everything I'd asked Him to do—which made me the object of my worship rather than Him.

I finally had to accept the reality that my circumstances do not alter His character. Anyone can say, "God is good" when wonderful things are happening. But God is holy and God is good no matter what we're going through.

Jesus talked about this very issue: "You fathers—if your children ask for a fish, do you give them a snake instead? Or if they ask for an egg, do you give them a scorpion? Of course not! So if you sinful people know how to give good gifts to your children, how much more will your heavenly Father give the Holy Spirit to those who ask him" (Luke 11:11-13).

Jesus said that God can't give us a bad gift, which is the opposite of how we feel when bad things happen. But now that I'm a dad, I think I have a deeper understanding of this passage than I used to. One of the things I absolutely love about being a father is seeing my daughter full of joy. But I also know that sometimes I have to intervene and tell her no or even step in and remove her from a situation that could harm her.

One morning when Charisse was about two years old, I walked into our kitchen and noticed her happily playing with something on the floor. I didn't think much of it and walked past her to make a cup of coffee. As I walked by again, I looked down to see what she was playing with. When I realized what it was, I nearly messed my pants.

She had spent the past several minutes playing with a live scorpion!

I don't know if you have ever seen one of these creatures, but I would say they closely resemble how I imagine Satan would look. They are nasty little animals whose venom can be poisonous and even deadly. They have claws that they use to seize their prey and stingers on their tails, which they use to hit their targets over and over. And the one on the floor was about to grab my daughter.

As a father who loves his little girl, I didn't hesitate for moment. I scooped her up as quickly as possible and slammed my foot on the scorpion so hard I'm sure it died twice! I then got a napkin, picked it up, and threw it in the sink, where I ground it up in the garbage disposal for about a minute to make sure the creation of Satan was chopped into as many pieces as possible.

After all of this was over, I put Charisse down and looked at her. I could see right away that she was angry—really angry—at me. With big tears in her eyes, she told me, "Daddy, you killed my friend."

In her mind, I was robbing her of her joy. I was hurting her. She couldn't see that what she thought of as my being mean was actually my rescuing her from future pain—which is exactly what our heavenly Father does for us.

God is holy, and God is good—and so are His desires for our lives. When we finally believe that His plans are greater than our plans, we can live in absolute freedom rather than being absolutely terrified of Him.

God is a good God who wants good things for His children.

Believe His Promises

I hate being by myself.

And I *really* hate being by myself at night. I grew up being scared of the dark, and on top of that, I had a dad who loved to jump out of the shadows and scare me.

When I was a kid I was petrified to be by myself and sleep in a dark room, except when I had a friend spend the night. Then I was great. I reasoned that if something did come out from under my bed to eat us, it would get my friend first, thus allowing me to escape.

While Lucretia and I were dating, she was attending medical school in Augusta, Georgia. Nearly every weekend I would drive down on Friday to see her. We would go out and get something to eat, and sometimes we'd hit a coffee shop or a movie. And then before I left to head back home, we'd go to this place in the downtown area where you could walk along the river. We'd often get there about eleven o'clock and walk around until midnight or so.

After we'd been doing this for several months, someone informed us that the area where we were hanging out wasn't the safest place. But I wasn't scared—not one bit—because Lucretia was with me.

I'm not joking. Here's the thing: Lucretia is a second-degree black belt in tae kwon do. In other words, she can kick some tail.

I told her one time that if three guys ever approached us and wanted my wallet, I'd take one of them and she could take the other two!

I wasn't scared—not because of what I could do, but because I knew the person with me was more powerful than I was. That gives me power by association.

With that image in mind, here's a promise each one of us needs to wrap our minds around: God is always with us. And He has more power than any bad guy we may come across in a dark alley.

One of the passages of Scripture I memorized early in my walk with Jesus was Isaiah 41:10:

Don't be afraid, for I am with you.
    Don't be discouraged, for I am your God.
I will strengthen you and help you.
    I will hold you up with my victorious right hand.

We don't have to be afraid, because He is with us!

The apostle Paul tells us, "Let your gentleness be evident to all. The Lord is near. Do not be anxious about anything, but in every situation, by prayer and petition, with thanksgiving, present your requests to God. And the peace of God, which transcends all understanding, will guard your hearts and your minds in Christ Jesus" (Philippians 4:5-7, NIV).

Notice that phrase "the Lord is near." The reason we don't have to be anxious about anything is because the Lord is near.

Why is it essential for us to understand that God is with us? Because God's presence is greater than our problems.

He has more power than we do.

He has more wisdom than we do.

He has more awareness than we do.

And if He is with us, we can walk through any stressful situation this world throws our way.

CHAPTER 11

LETTING GO OF CONTROL

Okay, it's time for a little survey. Do you have a type A personality? You are organized! You are detailed! You have color-coded calendars! You even color-coordinate your Skittles! You have a to-do list, and if that to-do list does not get to-doed, you absolutely lose it because you feel like your life is out of control.

I am a control freak when it comes to driving. I will hardly ever ride along in someone else's car. In the rare cases when I'm not driving, I often sit in a mild state of panic in the passenger's seat because the driver doesn't quite drive the way I would.

Maybe driving isn't the issue for you, but I'm guessing we all struggle with control in some area. And in God's goodness, I believe He constantly reminds us how little control we actually have!

Control is the greatest illusion in the universe.

Control is the greatest illusion in the universe. It's amazing how many of us have bought into the idea that we're in the driver's seat when in reality there are so many things we have no control over.

We didn't control when we were born.

We didn't control where we were born.

We didn't control what parents we were born to.

We can be the safest drivers in the world and have a very unsafe driver (whom we have no control over) run a red light and wreak havoc on us on our way to the grocery store.

We can eat organic and sign up for yoga and Pilates and be in amazing physical condition and still have a heart attack.

When we grasp how little control we have, it could make us want to hunker down in a room with no windows and doors. But if we understand that the God who is good and holy and always with us is in control, then our stress and anxiety levels will significantly decrease.

When we stop fighting for control, we can finally surrender to the One who is in control.

Who Are You Bowing Down To?

This is where we pick up our journey through the book of Daniel with his friends Shadrach, Meshach, and Abednego.

These guys ran into a bit of a tough situation—one full of potential stress and anxiety that could have absolutely crushed them. It all happened because King Nebuchadnezzar decided to build a statue of himself, one that was ninety feet tall and nine feet wide and made of solid gold.

As if that wasn't bold enough, he brought in a huge band and told the crowd that when the band began to play, everyone needed to bow down.

You may be thinking, *That's the dumbest idea I've ever heard. There's no way I would bow down to a statue of nutty Nebuchadnezzar.*

I'm with you, but there's one little detail about the decree we need to take note of: anyone who didn't bow down would be thrown into a blazing furnace.

It was simple, really: bow down and live, or don't bow and die.

Talk about your stress-filled situation.

Can you imagine being in these guys' shoes? When the decree is issued, you say to yourself, *There's no way I'm bowing,* but then the "or you'll die" section is added on. It would be easy to rationalize by saying, "Well, you know, I can bow on the outside but stand on the inside; after all, I need to try to stay alive."

Here we are, thousands of years later, and all of us still wrestle to some degree with that same pressure. The enemy is always going to put pressure on us, and if we're not careful, we begin to rationalize. I once heard someone say that when we rationalize, we tell "rational lies."

Your experience may go something like this:

Your boss comes in and asks you to do something that is clearly unethical. Here comes the tension—you know what you've been asked to do is wrong; however, if you don't do it, you may lose your job. All too often people fear unemployment more than they fear the Lord, and they "bow down" at work while planning on asking for forgiveness later.

Or let's say you're dating someone you shouldn't. You know what the Bible says about dating someone who is not following Jesus, but you fear being single more than you fear the Lord, so you rationalize.

The world is always going to pressure us to bow to something other than God because we feel that when we do, we are in control. But in fact, nothing could be further from the truth.

Back in Babylon, the band played and everyone bowed down . . . except for Shadrach, Meshach, and Abednego. They refused to bow because they knew that God is good, God is holy, God was with them, and God was in control.

If you refuse to bow down to false gods, you may experience stress and anxiety because you're going to stand out from the crowd. Try putting yourself in this scene:

At the sound of the musical instruments, all the people, whatever their race or nation or language, bowed to the ground and worshiped the gold statue that King Nebuchadnezzar had set up.

But some of the astrologers went to the king and informed on the Jews. They said to King Nebuchadnezzar, "Long live the king! You issued a decree requiring all the people to bow down and worship the gold statue when they hear the sound of the horn, flute, zither, lyre, harp, pipes, and other musical instruments. That decree also states that those who refuse to

obey must be thrown into a blazing furnace. But there are
some Jews—Shadrach, Meshach, and Abednego—whom you
have put in charge of the province of Babylon. They pay no
attention to you, Your Majesty. They refuse to serve your gods
and do not worship the gold statue you have set up."

DANIEL 3:7-12

Hundreds, possibly thousands of people bowed down—except for
three. They stood out like a group of senior adults at a Justin Bieber
concert!

As a result of their refusal, they faced an intense exchange with the
king:

Nebuchadnezzar flew into a rage and ordered that Shadrach,
Meshach, and Abednego be brought before him. When they
were brought in, Nebuchadnezzar said to them, "Is it true,
Shadrach, Meshach, and Abednego, that you refuse to serve my
gods or to worship the gold statue I have set up? I will give you
one more chance to bow down and worship the statue I have
made when you hear the sound of the musical instruments. But
if you refuse, you will be thrown immediately into the blazing
furnace. And then what god will be able to rescue you from my
power?"

DANIEL 3:13-15

Do you see what's happening here? King Nebuchadnezzar told them,
"Hey guys, I'm a little ticked at the fact that you stood up when everyone
else bowed down, so I'm going to give you another shot. After all, I'm a
fair guy. We're going to play this music one more time, and if you bow
down, then all is well. But if not, you're going to be thrown into the fire,
and nobody's going to save you."

The king pulled out all the stops here. Fear, intimidation, manipula-
tion—all weapons the enemy uses to bring stress and anxiety into our lives.

What Are You Focusing On?

Needless to say, these three guys were dealing with a situation that was unplanned and unprepared for. If they had decided to focus on their circumstances, they would have been crushed.

The same is true for us: we can get so focused on our circumstances that we can't focus on Christ.

That means we must make a choice: Will we focus on the size of our problem or the size of our God? The reality is, we can't do both.

Focusing on our circumstances and the size of our problems always leads to stress, anxiety, and fear. Focusing on Christ, however, allows us to walk in freedom.

And we really do have an enemy who is trying to keep us imprisoned. Jesus said Satan is the father of lies (see John 8:44) and that the enemy's goal is to steal, kill, and destroy us (see John 10:10). He will attack our minds, trying to get us to focus on all the things we have no control over.

> **Will we focus on the size of our problem or the size of our God?**

If you focus on the voice of the enemy, you will be controlled by fear. But if you are focused on the voice of God, you will be controlled by faith. There is no middle ground.

This is why it's absolutely essential to be grounded in God's Word. Only the truth of God's Word can shatter the lies of the enemy and cause stress and anxiety to fall from our shoulders like chains being removed from a prisoner's wrists.

Before Jesus began His public ministry, He went into the desert to be tempted by the devil (see Matthew 4; Luke 4). In His response to each temptation, He modeled how we can overcome anything the enemy throws at us. Jesus simply quoted the Bible back to the devil—something each one of us can do too.

Focusing on God's promises allows us to escape the potential prison that incorrect thinking can lead us to.

I learned this the hard way Christmas 2009.

As a pastor, I find that the easiest times to preach are Christmas and Easter. People show up all dressed up, and a pastor can say just about anything about Jesus and how He's the Savior of the world, and people will say it was the best thing they've ever heard.

That Christmas morning, before our first of multiple services, a couple of things happened to me that took my focus way off of Christ, and I began to obsess over some things I had no control over.

The more I worried, the deeper I sank into a feeling of hopelessness and despair. As the day went on, I sometimes felt like I could barely breathe from the weight on my chest.

That evening when it was time to preach for the final service, I walked onstage and began to deliver my message. Before I knew it, this thought flew into my mind: *Somebody in this room hates you.*

There was no one heckling me from the front row. No one had a T-shirt on that said "I hate preachers." People weren't getting up and walking out. I'm convinced that because I had been so unfocused and worried earlier in the day, I was an easy target for the enemy. Instead of dismissing the thought, as I might have on another day, I began to entertain it.

I started to think, *That's probably true. Someone in this room must hate me.* And since I didn't fight that thought with God's Word, the battle became even more intense in the minutes that followed.

A lot of people in this room hate you, the voice said.

Keep in mind that this was happening while I was preaching to hundreds of people. I was trying my best to keep it together, but I began to feel like I was holding on to a rope that was breaking.

Everybody in this room hates you, the voice went on.

And before I could think anything else, the voice threw in one more comment: *Someone is this room is about to kill you.*

I started sweating uncontrollably. My chest got so tight that I was sure I was having a heart attack. I was fighting to simply breathe and not pass out. It was my first experience with a full-blown panic attack. I had never experienced anything like it, and I just knew I was going to die.

I managed to finish the sermon and walk off the stage. I couldn't breathe or talk, and all the color had disappeared from my face. People were asking me if I was okay, and all I could think was, *I'm having a heart attack, and someone out there wants to kill me.* I couldn't even drive myself home that evening after the service.

When I got home, it took me about two hours to calm down. This was one of those situations when it was really convenient to have a medical doctor as a wife, and she was able to convince me I wasn't having a heart attack. I finally went to bed, and as I lay there reflecting on what had happened, I realized I had surrendered my thoughts to the enemy and allowed him to take me to a completely irrational place, resulting in a level of stress and anxiety I'd never before experienced.

Here's what the Bible says about our thought life: "We destroy every proud obstacle that keeps people from knowing God. We capture their rebellious thoughts and teach them to obey Christ" (2 Corinthians 10:5).

In other words, one of the few things we *do* have control over is what we choose to think about. The enemy doesn't want us to be focused on Christ or His Word. He wants us to focus on our circumstances. If he can get us focused on our circumstances, he can keep us in bondage to worry, fear, and anxiety.

What If There's No Rescue?

We see a remarkable response of confidence and faith in this next part of Shadrach, Meshach, and Abednego's story.

> Shadrach, Meshach, and Abednego replied, "O Nebuchadnezzar, we do not need to defend ourselves before you. If we are thrown into the blazing furnace, the God whom we serve is able to save us. He will rescue us from your power, Your Majesty."
> DANIEL 3:16-17

These guys were declaring that they believed God was greater than their circumstances. And this wasn't just nice words or a religious cliché. Take a look at their next statement: "But even if he doesn't, we want to make it clear to you, Your Majesty, that we will never serve your gods or worship the gold statue you have set up" (Daniel 3:18).

They knew that God was great and able, that God was holy and good, that God was in control and able to save them, but they clearly stated that even if He didn't rescue them, they still wouldn't bow down to the circumstances that were pressing against them.

I've never directed a movie, but if I were writing a script for this story, I believe this would be the perfect place for the rescue scene.

These guys just declared they weren't going to bow down even if it meant they had to die. I can see it now—the music begins to swell, the screen begins to transition from darkness to light, and all of a sudden some redneck angels bust onto the scene and tear up the place!

But it didn't happen that way. God didn't come swooping in.

No white horse.

No heroic rescue.

No action-adventure scene.

Nope! In fact, quite the opposite takes place.

Daniel 3:19 says, "Nebuchadnezzar was so furious with Shadrach, Meshach, and Abednego that his face became distorted with rage. He commanded that the furnace be heated seven times hotter than usual."

Seven times hotter.

Don't miss that—it's huge!

So often I've thought that if I said all the right things or did the right things, my life would get easier.

Isn't that what religion teaches? As long as we do everything just right, nothing bad will ever happen to us!

But Shadrach, Meshach, and Abednego had done all the right things—they had stood their ground and believed that God was greater than what they were going through—and now they were on their way to a furnace that was seven times hotter than it was before.

Some of us may have to walk into a furnace that is seven times hotter than we expected before we come out of our trial.

It may get seven times hotter at work tomorrow.

It may get seven times hotter in your difficult marriage.

It may get seven times hotter in your relationship with your parents or your children.

> [The king] ordered some of the strongest men of his army to bind Shadrach, Meshach, and Abednego and throw them into the blazing furnace. So they tied them up and threw them into the furnace, fully dressed in their pants, turbans, robes, and other garments. And because the king, in his anger, had demanded such a hot fire in the furnace, the flames killed the soldiers as they threw the three men in. So Shadrach, Meshach, and Abednego, securely tied, fell into the roaring flames.
>
> DANIEL 3:20-23

They'd done everything right, and God still allowed them to go into the furnace.

What about God being holy?

What about God being good?

What about God being with them?

What about God being in control?

Just because we follow Jesus, it doesn't mean we escape stressful and anxiety-filled circumstances.

But the three friends' story isn't over yet—and neither is yours!

CHAPTER 12

COMING OUT OF THE FIRE UNHARMED

I'd like to take a moment to fill you in on a kitchen tip from the Noble household. When it comes to our pantry, Lucretia knows everything that is in there—I mean *everything*. She knows which side of the pantry something is on, what shelf it's on, and what color the box or bag is.

I, on the other hand, know where nothing is!

One evening I was seriously craving club crackers. Not your plain-Jane saltines, but the good ones—the ones that are completely fattening, unhealthy, and made with lots of real butter. The kind Chick-fil-A restaurants used to put out along with all their condiments but had to stop because people would grab handfuls and put them in their pockets. (If you just laughed, it's because you're guilty!)

I asked Lucretia if we had any, and she told me they were in the pantry. I opened the door and began looking . . . and looking . . . and looking. I stood there for what seemed like an eternity and combed every inch of the space. There were no club crackers to be found.

I finally told her, "They're not in here—you must be mistaken."

"Look on the third shelf about halfway over," she fired back. "The big green box—you can't miss them."

I was missing them because they weren't there! "Well, someone must have broken into our house and stolen our club crackers," I said. "We need to call the cops, because they're not here."

At this point Lucretia walked over to the pantry, grabbed the box of club crackers, and handed them to me. (I still think she had them hidden behind her back the whole time.) And then she gave me a smile that said, "I really do love you . . . but you're as dumb as a rock!"

I learned a valuable lesson that day: you see what you're prepared to see.

Open Your Eyes

If we aren't careful, we will allow the world to press us into its mold. Before long, instead of seeing things through God's eyes, we start seeing the worst in every person and every situation.

When God shows up, however, He changes everything, including our perceptions. We don't have to stay stuck seeing only what the world tells us we should expect to see.

Let's dive back into Daniel's story:

> Suddenly, Nebuchadnezzar jumped up in amazement and exclaimed to his advisers, "Didn't we tie up three men and throw them into the furnace?"
>
> "Yes, Your Majesty, we certainly did," they replied.
>
> "Look!" Nebuchadnezzar shouted. "I see four men, unbound, walking around in the fire unharmed! And the fourth looks like a god!"
>
> DANIEL 3:24-25

Nebuchadnezzar was ready to gloat.

Nebuchadnezzar thought he had won.

Nebuchadnezzar was most likely sitting there expecting to hear screams of torment and men begging for mercy.

But all of a sudden he leaped to his feet in amazement. It's important to understand that in that culture, men of importance didn't leap to their feet for anything. The very fact that the king did so meant something unbelievable was taking place.

Now I'm not sure how he saw all this—maybe he had a JumboTron set up or maybe it was the angle he was sitting at—but he saw the men he'd thrown into the fire walking around unbound and unharmed. And if that wasn't enough to freak him out, he was shocked to see a fourth guy in the fire.

Nebuchadnezzar was prepared to see destruction. He wasn't prepared to see God move!

Most Bible experts agree that the fourth man in the fire was an Old Testament appearance of Jesus Christ. But Shadrach, Meshach, and Abednego didn't see Jesus until they got into the fire. If you're in the middle of circumstances that are creating intense amounts of stress and anxiety in you—circumstances that seem seven times hotter than anything you've ever gone through—then it may be time to stop praying, "God, get me out of this" and begin praying, "Jesus, let me see You."

When we see Jesus clearly, we will follow Him closely. However, we often won't see Him clearly until we've been thrown into the middle of a fire that is seven times hotter than anything we've ever experienced.

Jesus gets our attention in the fire in ways we never would have noticed if things were always good in our lives. That's what He did with these three guys in the story—and that's what He has done over and over again in my own life. Every time I've walked through the fire, He has allowed me to do so in order for me to see Him more clearly and follow Him more closely.

> It may be time to stop praying, "God, get me out of this" and begin praying, "Jesus, let me see You."

How would we know He's a healer if we didn't experience times when we needed to be healed?

How would we know He's a Savior if we didn't experience things we needed to be saved from?

How would we know He's a provider if we didn't experience times when we thought we weren't going to make it?

If you feel like you're walking in a fire that's seven times hotter than anything you've ever experienced, my challenge to you is to pray this bold prayer: "Jesus, let me see You. Teach me who You are in this fire."

And then open your eyes, because He is there. How do I know? Because He is holy and He is good, He promised to always be with us, and He is in complete control. All we need to do is open our eyes.

Embrace Freedom

Have you ever changed your mind about something? If you are a married man, then the answer is a resounding "Yes!"

For example, I used to think it was perfectly acceptable for a dirty towel to make itself at home on the bedroom floor for a month or so; however, after marriage, I was informed that dirty towels on the floor would equal tension in my life.

I changed!

Let's take a look at King Nebuchadnezzar's change of heart.

Nebuchadnezzar came as close as he could to the door of the flaming furnace and shouted: "Shadrach, Meshach, and Abednego, servants of the Most High God, come out! Come here!"

So Shadrach, Meshach, and Abednego stepped out of the fire.

DANIEL 3:26

Nebuchadnezzar went from saying, "What god will be able to rescue you?" to referring to the Lord as "the Most High God." Talk about the power of a testimony.

One thing that's essential for followers of Jesus to understand is that non-Christians are watching the way we walk through the fire. And the way we respond to the flames that are thrown at us can teach people way more about Jesus than any sermon or lecture ever could.

If we will walk through the fire with the assurance that Jesus is with us, then people who don't know Him will pay attention.

> The high officers, officials, governors, and advisers crowded
> around them and saw that the fire had not touched them. Not
> a hair on their heads was singed, and their clothing was not
> scorched. They didn't even smell of smoke!
>
> DANIEL 3:27

Did you catch that? Not a hair on their heads was singed. If you've ever been around someone who used a curling iron or a flat iron, you know this is a miracle. They had just walked through fire and their hair was still in place when it was over!

Perhaps even more amazing to me is that "there was no smell of fire on them."

I live in the southeastern part of the United States, and many of the restaurants here still have smoking and nonsmoking sections. It drives me absolutely insane! I always request the nonsmoking section, but sometimes the hostess seats me right beside the smoking section.

Uh, it doesn't work! Saying that there is a no-smoking section in a restaurant is like saying there is a no-peeing section in a pool.

Smoke travels, and when it lands on you, you are going to smell like smoke for the rest of the day. And since my wife has really long hair, it takes about eighteen hours in the shower to get the smell out.

So think about this for a second: it wasn't like Shadrach, Meshach, and Abednego were in a restaurant sitting in the smoking section—they were in a furnace with real smoke and fire, and the Bible says they didn't even smell like smoke. God is more powerful than we can grasp . . . and He proves it by handling what some would consider the smallest detail.

The smallest details in our lives are a big deal to the God who loves us.

There's one more thing I want to note about this part of the story.

> "Look!" Nebuchadnezzar shouted. "I see four men, unbound,
> walking around in the fire unharmed! And the fourth looks like
> a god!"
>
> DANIEL 3:25

The Bible clearly states that the men went into the furnace tied up, but they came out of the furnace unbound. The only thing that was burned off of them in the furnace is what the enemy used to tie them down.

The same is true for us. God wants to use the fire to remove whatever the enemy has been using to hold us back. The enemy tries to bind us up and put us in a place of destruction. But like these men in the furnace, we can come out of the fire unbound!

Nebuchadnezzar said, "Praise to the God of Shadrach, Meshach, and Abednego! He sent his angel to rescue his servants who trusted in him. They defied the king's command and were willing to die rather than serve or worship any god except their own God. Therefore, I make this decree: If any people, whatever their race or nation or language, speak a word against the God of Shadrach, Meshach, and Abednego, they will be torn limb from limb, and their houses will be turned into heaps of rubble. There is no other god who can rescue like this!"

Then the king promoted Shadrach, Meshach, and Abednego to even higher positions in the province of Babylon.

DANIEL 3:28-30

So often we believe (sometimes as a result of really bad Bible teaching) that we go through the fire because God is punishing us. But we see in this story that the purpose of the fire is not punishment but promotion.

When we can fully explain God, He ceases to be God.

I don't understand how God can use bad things for good. I don't understand a lot of things about God. But when we can fully explain God, He ceases to be God. All I know is that He took a bloodstained cross and turned it into an empty tomb, and a God who can do that is worthy of my worship and my trust.

Where Is Jesus?

Before we conclude this chapter, it's essential for us to understand one more thing. First, let's do a quick recap.

How many men went into the fire? *Three.*

How many men were seen in the fire? *Four.*

Who was that fourth man? *Jesus.*

How many men came out of the fire? *Three.*

Then where is Jesus? *He's still in the fire!*

The book of Isaiah gives us these words of encouragement about our overwhelming circumstances:

> O Jacob, listen to the LORD who created you.
>   O Israel, the one who formed you says,
> "Do not be afraid, for I have ransomed you.
>   I have called you by name; you are mine.
> When you go through deep waters,
>   I will be with you.
> When you go through rivers of difficulty,
>   you will not drown.
> When you walk through the fire of oppression,
>   you will not be burned up;
>   the flames will not consume you.
> For I am the LORD, your God,
>   the Holy One of Israel, your Savior.

ISAIAH 43:1-3

We will not be burned in the fire because He is in the fire Himself. He will walk with us through whatever flames we have to journey through.

When my mother passed away, my twelve-year-old self had no resources to deal with something so life shattering. But about three months after she died, a woman who was close to our family offered me some words of encouragement I've never forgotten. She was with my mother when she died, and she told me the story of what happened that night.

"Perry," she told me, "in the last few hours of life, your mom really did suffer. The cancer was causing her intense pain, and there was nothing the doctors could do. She struggled to breathe. She was writhing in pain. And about an hour or so before she died, she passed out.

"Then, about a minute or so before she passed away, your mother opened her eyes and her face lit up. She smiled bigger than she'd ever smiled before and reached out both hands toward the ceiling. I asked her what was happening, and she said, 'Don't you see Him? Don't you see Him? It's Jesus!'

"I asked what He looked like, and your mother simply said, 'He's beautiful!' And then she put her head on her pillow and died."

Here's what I absolutely love about that story: when my mother passed away, she didn't step into the arms of a stranger but rather the arms of her Savior. In what the world would call her darkest moment—when other people would say her life was at its most hopeless point—Jesus revealed Himself to her. She didn't have to fear death because she had seen the Author of life on the other side.

The Jesus my mother saw in the hospital room that night is the same Jesus who has told us, "I am with you. I love you. I will never leave you. I am holy. I am good. I am in control. And all I want you to do is open your eyes and see Me so you can embrace the freedom I've called you to walk in."

We will never be free of stress until we see the Savior. Period. But when we open our eyes and see Him, we will follow Him wherever He goes because we know we can go through whatever He leads us to—even if it's a fiery furnace.

CHAPTER 13

STICKY
NOTES

What would you say are the greatest inventions of all time? I have several suggestions.

Electricity would have to be at the top of the list. I'm thankful that when the sun went down last night I didn't have to light a candle to see and instead was able to flip on a switch and *poof!*, my house had light.

I believe the iPod is an incredible invention too. (Anyone remember trying to work out in the gym with a portable CD player?)

The remote control changed my life—literally. Why? Because until the remote control came along, my father used me as the remote control! Every time he got bored with a TV show, he'd bark at me to change the channel. Needless to say, I was relieved when I didn't have to be the human remote anymore.

All that said, however, I believe that one of the greatest inventions of all time is the sticky note.

Some of you may be nodding in agreement right now. Others may be scratching your heads, wondering if I am smoking crack, so allow me to explain.

I have a tendency to forget things.

I don't mean to, but when I get focused on one thing, I tend to lose sight of other things that are important. (One time when my daughter was about nine months old, I packed up her diaper bag and all the accessories needed to take a child out of the house, and when I finally got in the car, I realized that while I'd remembered all her stuff, I'd left her in the house in her carrier seat!)

Sticky notes are an incredible tool that I use to remind me of what is really important.

When I need to remember something important, I write it on a sticky note. I've found that putting this reminder in a place where I can see it often helps me focus on what's most important. My office has sticky notes all over it. I am hardly ever without a pack of them on me.

Similarly in our spiritual lives, most of us would agree that we have a short memory when it comes to truths about God. We tend to forget even some of the most significant things God has revealed to us. That's why He gives us reminders—divine sticky notes—to point us back to His love. He knows that the moment we forget how much He loves us is precisely when we're most vulnerable to feeling overwhelmed.

Reminders of His Love

No matter how good you are, no matter how long you've been a Christian, no matter how much of the Bible you know, there will be times in your life when you struggle to believe in God's love.

This struggle doesn't mean you're a bad person; it merely confirms that you're a human being.

For example, it's often hard to believe in God's love when we ask Him to heal someone we love who's physically sick and He doesn't do it. Situations like these can bring on anxiety as we ask ourselves questions like *Is this my fault? Did I not have enough faith? Does God not do this kind of thing anymore?*

Or if you have a past that dominates your thoughts, you may find it hard to believe that God loves you. I've fought this battle myself. The way I lived my life before I met Jesus wasn't pretty. And if I allow myself to obsess over who I was rather than focus on who I am in Christ, I can convince myself that God probably loves everyone else except me.

Focusing on my past has even caused me to doubt my own salvation at times, which has caused me immense stress.

Sometimes we doubt God's love when our circumstances seem to be out of control. I've been in the middle of difficult situations and found myself asking, "If God is good and He's in control, then how in the world could He allow this to happen to me?"

Other times we doubt God's love when we can't seem to quit committing the same sin over and over again. I've had people ask me, "How in the world could God

> What gets our attention will ultimately determine our direction.

love me? I mess up, I ask for forgiveness, and then I do it again. I want to stop, but I don't know how. God probably is so frustrated with me that He doesn't want anything to do with me anymore."

Every one of us has battled with whether God loves us.

In my struggles with this issue, I finally grasped that facts are greater than how we feel. If we allow our feelings to determine what we think and how we behave, we will never escape the pit of despair and hopelessness that anxiety places us in. However, if we allow our minds to be shaped by facts, we can live a life that is full of hope and peace, despite our circumstances.

Getting Our Attention

When I was reading the first few chapters of Daniel, I discovered something that blew my mind.

This theme runs through the entire book: what gets our attention will ultimately determine our direction. If we are obsessed with stressful circumstances, we will constantly be overwhelmed. But if we are obsessed with Christ, we will overcome.

In the first four chapters of Daniel, we see that God really is serious about getting our attention. And that truth comes across most clearly not in Daniel's story but in someone else's.

Stay with me here.

Daniel isn't even mentioned in chapter 3—the story of Shadrach, Meshach, and Abednego. And while Shadrach, Meshach, and Abednego are mentioned in chapters 1–3, they don't appear in chapter 4 (or the rest of the book, for that matter).

However, there is one character who makes an appearance in each of the first four chapters: King Nebuchadnezzar.

Now I'm not saying we should rename the book Nebuchadnezzar, but I do think the commentary about him in these chapters gives us a lot to think about when it comes to knowing that God really does love us.

I believe Nebuchadnezzar had four "sticky notes" he couldn't get away from that finally led him to acknowledge the one true God. He couldn't escape the fact that God loved him and was pursuing him. And there's good news for us: those same four reminders are true for all of us today.

CHAPTER 14

REMINDER #1: CREATION

I absolutely love to travel.

Getting on an airplane to go to other parts of the world sets my soul on fire. I love to see and experience new things. And when I do, I'm reminded that God is so much bigger than I give Him credit for.

As our view of God increases, our worry and stress decrease, because it's only then that we begin to believe that all the things that are over our heads are under His feet.

Nebuchadnezzar was king of what was, at the time, the largest empire in the world, which meant he had some significant military responsibilities. Today if a country declares war on another country, the leaders of those nations don't actually place themselves in the combat situation but instead sign some sort of executive order and focus on the diplomatic side of things. But back in Nebuchadnezzar's time, when an army went to war, the king not only went out with them, but he also led them into battle.

Because of the size and scope of Nebuchadnezzar's empire, he was likely able to travel a good bit. He had the opportunity to see things he'd never seen. He was exposed to new experiences. He must have been constantly reminded that the world was so much bigger than he was, and I would argue that he was also reminded that there was Someone out there who was bigger than he was.

The Bible captures this idea in one of the psalms:

> The heavens proclaim the glory of God.
>> The skies display his craftsmanship.
> Day after day they continue to speak;
>> night after night they make him known.
> They speak without a sound or word;
>> their voice is never heard.
> Yet their message has gone throughout the earth,
>> and their words to all the world.

PSALM 19:1-4

God has made Himself obvious to us through His creation.

I remember the first time I went to Jackson Hole, Wyoming, to see the Grand Tetons. When I stood at the base of those enormous mountains, I didn't have the thought, *Wow, I am really awesome!* Nope. I understood that God was awesome, God was huge, and I was very small—and so was everything I was going through.

All the things that are over our heads are under His feet.

Another experience comes to mind—one day in particular when I became aware of how amazing and huge God is. That was the day my daughter was born.

Some people say the birth of a child is the most beautiful thing they have ever seen. I beg to differ.

It wasn't beautiful. It freaked me out!

They gave Lucretia drugs but refused to give them to me! (Yes, I asked.)

I was nervous.

I felt like I was going to pass out.

I felt helpless and completely out of control.

Then I saw Charisse for the first time, and I was reminded of the greatness of our Creator.

I've heard this argument from different people over the years: "Perry, here's the deal. Creation is great. The mountains are beautiful. Outer space is amazing. The birth of a baby is incredible. But all those things are the result of chaos. We exist because of random chance. An explosion happened millions of years ago that produced one cell. Then one cell decided to become two. Two became four, and four became a tadpole. The tadpole turned into a frog. The frog turned into a bunny. The bunny hopped up a tree and turned into a monkey. The monkey then went to Walmart, bought a razor, and shaved, and that's how humankind came to be."

I'm not trying to pick a fight, but believing that the entire universe, this planet, and even the person you saw in the mirror this morning are all here because of random cosmic activity is not consistent with rational thinking. Design by its very nature implies that there has to be a designer.

Let me explain by talking about one of my favorite things in the entire world: cupcakes.

We have a cupcake store in upstate South Carolina that makes cupcakes so amazing they will make you want to smack your grandma! (That's Southern for "They are really good!")

One of my favorite cupcakes of all time is their chocolate chip cupcake.

It's hard to even put it into words, but I'll do my best. When you look at it, you see a perfectly rounded chocolate cupcake with lots of chocolate frosting swirled around and around on it. You get a sugar rush that lasts for two weeks just from the icing.

Then there are chocolate chips sprinkled all over the frosting and a huge Hershey's Kiss right on top.

But it doesn't stop there! When you break open the cupcake, you discover that the inside is full of the most amazing chocolate mousse you've ever put in your mouth.

Want one? I sure do!

These cupcakes are the product of someone who put thought, time, and preparation into making them.

They are intentional, not accidental!

No one in the world would claim that these cupcakes were made by chance when someone lit a stick of dynamite and threw it into a bakery, resulting in a massive explosion that threw all the right ingredients together at just the right time to produce a fully formed, delicious cupcake.

I will say it again: design implies a designer.

The Grand Tetons are not accidental; they are intentional.

The universe is not accidental; it is intentional.

Human life is not accidental; it is intentional.

Which means that you are not an accident! You were custom-designed by the Creator of the universe.

And the same God uses creation as His megaphone to let us get a glimpse into His character and His love for us. The apostle Paul puts it this way: "Ever since the world was created, people have seen the earth and sky. Through everything God made, they can clearly see his invisible qualities—his eternal power and divine nature. So they have no excuse for not knowing God" (Romans 1:20).

This is a truth we need to soak in if we are ever going to overcome those overwhelmed feelings that plague us. If we truly grasp that *the* God who created everything is also in charge of our own struggles, we'll be able to get a better perspective on the things we're facing.

Several years ago, Lucretia and I were on a vacation, and I woke up early one morning. Honestly, I was a little angry at the time—after all, I was on vacation, and I was looking forward to some good sleep.

The room we were staying in was on the ocean, so I got up and peeked out the window. I stood there, stunned, as the sun broke over the horizon. It was one of the most beautiful things I have ever seen. The horizon exploded in breathtaking colors of red, yellow, pink, and orange. I couldn't move and struggled to catch my breath as I was overcome by the magnificence of that moment. Immediately after I saw that incredible sunrise, I was reminded of this Scripture passage:

The faithful love of the LORD never ends!
His mercies never cease.
Great is his faithfulness;
his mercies begin afresh each morning.

LAMENTATIONS 3:22-23

The next time you see a sunrise, remind yourself, *God is faithful.*

The next time you see snow-covered mountains with their peaks pointing toward the sky, remind yourself, *God is faithful.*

The next time you see flowers that have burst into bloom because winter couldn't stop them from developing in the hidden places, remind yourself, *God is faithful.*

The next time you hold a soft-skinned baby in your arms, remind yourself, *God is faithful.*

Creation is one of God's amazing reminders that our God is much bigger than we can imagine and that He can handle anything we are going through.

CHAPTER 15

REMINDER #2: THE PEOPLE WE MEET

"The people I meet . . ." If you just read that phrase and started singing, "always go their separate ways," then I know you were alive in the '80s and listened to Bon Jovi! (If you don't know what I'm talking about, then it's high time to Google the song.)

I enrolled in Anderson College (now Anderson University) in the fall of 1990. During the fall semester of my freshman year, I met a girl named Christine. One day at lunch she said, "Perry, why are you in college? What do you want to do when you graduate?"

"I want to be a preacher," I said.

"Oh, wow," she replied. "My daddy is in the ministry."

"What does he do?"

"He works with people to help them plant new churches," she said.

I thought, *That's the dumbest thing I've ever heard in my life.* I didn't say that out loud, though, because I thought she was hot and was trying to get a date.

Honestly, I'd never heard of anything like church planting before. And having grown up in the southeastern part of the United States, I knew there were plenty of churches around. Why start another one?

Fast-forward six years. Through a series of undeniable circumstances,

I started to feel the Lord impressing on me that He wanted me to start a church one day. I was okay with that, because I thought He wouldn't ask me to do anything with that calling until I was fifty or sixty years old.

But in 1999 that thought was shattered when the Lord led me to put the pieces in place to start NewSpring Church.

I had no idea what I was doing. At the time, there were hardly any books on the subject of church planting, and I didn't know many people who had actually tried it. So I contacted a church-planting organization and was put in touch with a man by the name of Norman.

Over lunch together, Norman and I started getting to know each other. He asked me to tell him a little bit about myself, including where I'd attended college.

I told him I'd graduated from Anderson College. When I told him I'd started there in 1990, he interrupted me, "My daughter was there in 1990."

"What was her name?" I asked.

You've probably already guessed—it was Christine! The Lord used what I had considered to be an unimportant relationship years before (because she wouldn't go out with me) to significantly impact my life nine years later through her father.

You have never met a person by accident. Never!

Every relationship you've ever had has passed through the hands of God.

Let's take a moment to talk about Nebuchadnezzar again. He was one of the most powerful men in the world at the time. He was a king, a world ruler, a dictator of a powerful nation. And yet in Daniel 1, he established a relationship with Daniel, Shadrach, Meshach, and Abednego—four young guys who had been captured to serve as slaves.

Scripture doesn't explicitly say this, but I have to believe these relationships were a major reason Nebuchadnezzar was able to finally get a true picture of the Lord's character. Nebuchadnezzar met these guys in chapter 1, he saw them do the impossible in chapter 2, and he watched three of them defy death by overcoming insurmountable circumstances in chapter 3. These encounters no doubt had a profound impact on his life, leading up to his proclamation about the one true God: "There is no other god who can rescue like this!" (Daniel 3:29).

Whenever I'm doubting whether God cares about me and loves me, I take a look at the people He has placed in my life, and I'm always reminded that He cares about me even more than I care about myself at times.

I can still remember meeting David.

David sat right in front of me in English class my junior year of high school. He and I chatted nearly every day; however, when he began talking to me about going to church with him, I immediately shut down the conversation. He kept up the invites all year, and I kept ignoring him and making excuses. There was no way I was going to church. I was angry, bitter, and confused about God, and I'd concluded that the best thing to do was walk away from Him.

> **You have never met a person by accident.**

Then the summer of 1988 hit, and it felt like my life was unraveling. My dad was arrested for selling drugs, and for a time, I had no place to live. Life as I knew it was over, and this new season was unfamiliar and frightening.

During my senior year, I didn't have any classes with David, but I saw him from time to time at lunch. He was always really nice to me, and he told me that if I ever wanted to go to church with him, he'd be glad to take me.

I always refused, but while I found him annoying at times, the Lord used David to begin tugging on my heart.

Finally David switched tactics. He had accepted that I wasn't going to go to church, but he knew I loved to play pickup basketball. So one day he invited me to a Bible study. I was about to lower the boom on him for even thinking I'd attend his stupid Bible study until he told me, "We always play basketball after Bible study, and there are really hot girls who stay around to watch."

All of a sudden I was really interested in studying the Bible (despite the fact that I wasn't sure where mine was!).

I showed up the following Monday night, and although I didn't care much about God, Jesus, church, or the Bible, something kept drawing me back. David invited me the next week too, and I went again. In fact, I hardly missed a night. After he had me at Bible study, it wasn't long before I was going to church, and soon after, on May 27, 1990, I surrendered my life to Jesus.

Whenever I doubt God's love for me, I think back to my junior year in high school and how He placed a guy in front of me in English class as part of His plan to pursue me.

I'll bet as you look back on your own life, you can list people who have impacted your spiritual journey too.

Maybe there was someone who helped you wrestle through an issue.

Someone who stood by your side during a difficult time.

Someone who sent you a text out of the blue, letting you know they were thinking about you.

Someone God used to help open your heart toward Him.

Not a single one of those relationships was accidental. God hasn't left us alone—He has offered His own presence as well as other people to walk with us through whatever we're going through.

I challenge you to take a few moments to think back on the people God has brought into your life.

Who just happened to be there for you when your life was falling apart?

Who kept inviting you to church and wouldn't take no for an answer?

Who called you just when you thought everyone had given up on you?

God uses people in our lives to remind us that He loves us and that He will never leave us alone in our overwhelming circumstances.

CHAPTER 16

REMINDER #3: THE CIRCUMSTANCES WE GO THROUGH

Recently Lucretia, Charisse, and I went to visit Lucretia's parents in Thomasville, Georgia.

Now before I get into this story, let me just say that based on my observations, grandchildren absolutely change a person's life. People say there's something special about a grandchild that changes your perspective, and my family and I were about to find that out firsthand.

Lucretia had grown up in a strict home. Not necessarily a mean home, but a strict one nonetheless. Her parents' statements were not options to be considered; they were commands to be followed. And according to my wife, one of the strictest commands was that there was no jumping on the bed.

My wife found this rule to be a bit restrictive when she was a little girl, and she felt she had a valid reason to break it. She'd always wanted a trampoline, but her parents wouldn't buy one for her. The conclusion she came to was that if she couldn't have a trampoline, then she should be allowed to jump on the bed. Lucretia would say that the most trouble she ever got into when she was little was for jumping on the bed.

So today, in our house, there is no jumping on the bed.

Charisse is not allowed to jump on the bed.

I am not allowed to jump on the bed.

No one is!

So, with this in mind, let's return to what has become known as the bed-jumping incident.

When we arrived at my in-laws' house, the three of us headed upstairs with Lucretia's mother to the room we'd be staying in, which had a king-size bed. I'm not quite sure why, but as soon as Charisse saw the huge bed, she shrieked with joy, climbed on it, and began jumping like crazy.

Lucretia immediately said, "Charisse, no-no-no, you know we don't jump on the bed!" I'm sure having her mother right beside her made the situation extra tense.

Only in Christ can the victim walk in victory!

That's when Lucretia's mother said, "Let her jump on that bed if she wants. It's all right. She's not going to hurt anything."

Lucretia's eyes became as big around as saucers. She gave her mother a shocked look and said, "Who are you?"

At that point I did what any man with common sense would do in such a situation. I left the room!

I'm not entirely sure what happened to bring about this change. (Lucretia still won't let me jump on the bed.) But I'm sure that my mother-in-law was changed by her new circumstances. She saw things differently as a grandmother than she did as a mother.

Circumstances change us.

Going from being single to being married changes us.

Going from having no kids to being parents changes us.

Getting older changes us.

Moving to a new place changes us.

Getting a new job changes us.

Everything that happens to us changes us—for the good or for the bad. But it's impossible to remain unchanged by our circumstances.

Nebuchadnezzar went through some completely amazing circumstances that changed him, too.

In the first chapter of Daniel, we read about his plans for shaping and developing the Israelites in captivity and how those plans didn't work out according to what he'd had in mind.

In chapter 2, we read about his disturbing dream that caused him to doubt everyone around him.

Chapter 3 tells about the time he was an eyewitness to a miracle and how that circumstance made him start thinking differently about the one true God.

When Nebuchadnezzar finally worshiped the Lord, I believe his change of heart came in large part due to the circumstances he had gone through. "My sanity returned, and I praised and worshiped the Most High and honored the one who lives forever" (Daniel 4:34).

God uses circumstances to get our attention—sometimes good ones, sometimes bad ones. But He always uses them for our good.

I've been in ministry for more than twenty years. During that time I've heard hundreds of people tell me what the Lord used to get their attention. Here are just a few of the responses I've heard:

"When I was told I had cancer, the Lord had my attention."

"When my child was born, the Lord had my attention."

"When I went through a divorce, the Lord had my attention."

"When God showed Himself to me after I asked if He was real, He had my attention."

I have met so many people who have faced life-altering situations that the Lord used to get their attention. And I have seen Him bring people through these circumstances and into a greater understanding of who He is.

Only in Christ can the victim walk in victory!

You may be going through a set of circumstances that are completely overwhelming right now. I know from personal experience that when we find ourselves in the middle of situations like these, we tend to feel confused, frustrated, and alone.

However, as I look back on some of the most painful circumstances in my past, such as losing my mother and my father, I can see that during the times I thought God was far from me and didn't care about my pain, He was actually closer to me than ever before, guiding me through my struggles.

Anytime I have trouble believing God is able to handle what I'm going through, I look back on His faithfulness in the past, and that gives me strength to keep pressing on for the future.

During my most intense battles with stress and anxiety, I have found that freedom from my circumstances begins when I focus on Christ, knowing He is so much greater than what I am going through.

Jesus is greater than divorce.

Jesus is greater than cancer.

Jesus is greater than a past that haunts you.

Jesus is greater than an uncertain future.

Whatever you're facing, Jesus is greater! Those times when we walk through the valley of the shadow of death can be precious, because they remind us that He is the author of life.

CHAPTER 17

REMINDER #4: JESUS

Before I was married, I lived in the upstairs apartment of an apartment building. There was a guy who lived right below me, and for some reason I didn't like him.

I don't know why—he never said anything mean to me, and he always had a smile on his face. But the more I saw him, the more I just couldn't stand him.

One day when I pulled into the parking lot of the apartment complex, the only place to park was right beside him, which wouldn't have been a problem except that he had his hood up and was working on his car.

I pulled in and tried to sort of sneak out of my car so I wouldn't have to talk to him, but almost immediately he looked out from under his car hood and said hello. I was trapped—I had to say something. Before I had a chance to stop myself, the dumbest thing I could have said came flying out of my mouth.

"Uh . . . are you working on your car?"

At this point he could have hammered me about asking dumb questions, but instead he said, "I'm just cleaning my battery cables."

We stood there awkwardly for a few seconds, and then I managed to blurt out, "Well, uh, I think I need to clean mine, too."

He smiled at me. "If you pop your hood, I'll clean them for you."

"Huh?"

"Yeah, just open your hood," he said. "I'd love to do that for you, man."

I wasn't sure what to do at that point. Here was a guy I didn't like offering to do something nice for me. I opened the hood to see what would happen, and he spent the next five to ten minutes cleaning my battery cables.

I thanked him and walked into my apartment, where I felt the Holy Spirit asking me, "So, how does that feel?"

Two thoughts entered my mind in that moment. The first was that I really hoped that the next time I pulled into a parking spot next to my neighbor, he'd be washing his car. The second thought was that I had completely misjudged this guy and I'd been wrong in doing so.

We've all misjudged other people in some capacity before. We decide we don't like someone because of who they're associated with, what we've heard about them, or the misconceptions we have about their character.

And many times we do the same thing with Jesus.

When I first became a Christian and heard people talk about Jesus being the answer to all of life's hurts and disappointments, I concluded that Christians were way too simplistic. I'd been hurt, and while I was convinced that God loved me, I wasn't too sure about Jesus.

And then I got to know Him better.

Sure enough, I'd misjudged Him, just as I'd misjudged my neighbor.

I've had people tell me they don't like Jesus because most of the people who claim to be Christians are crazy.

I always give the same answer: "We *are* all crazy—all of us!" We do and say really dumb things sometimes.

None of us are perfect.

We fight and argue way more than we should.

We point our fingers at other people's sins when we should be looking at our own. Which is why I try to direct people's focus onto the person of Jesus Christ as He is revealed in Scripture rather than on the behavior of the "saints."

When the true Jesus reveals Himself to you, you can't stay the way you are; you will be changed. Jesus always changes people. No one who has ever met Him and acknowledged Him as Lord has ever walked away the same.

Of all the reminders God has given us of His love, Jesus is our greatest reminder. Anytime I feel beaten up by life's overwhelming circumstances and doubt God's ability to handle what I'm going through, I take courage by focusing on Jesus.

King Nebuchadnezzar had an interesting experience of focusing on Jesus too. Let's go back to the story of Shadrach, Meshach, and Abednego in the fiery furnace.

> **When the true Jesus reveals Himself to you, you can't stay the way you are; you will be changed.**

Suddenly, Nebuchadnezzar jumped up in amazement and exclaimed to his advisers, "Didn't we tie up three men and throw them into the furnace?"

"Yes, Your Majesty, we certainly did," they replied.

"Look!" Nebuchadnezzar shouted. "I see four men, unbound, walking around in the fire unharmed! And the fourth looks like a god!"

DANIEL 3:24-25

Nebuchadnezzar wasn't looking at Shadrach, Meshach, or Abednego. His eyes were focused on the fourth guy.

He saw Jesus!

And when he saw Him, he didn't say, "Hey, who's the guy with the golden sash and feathered hair walking around handing out lollipops and giving everyone a hug?" He leaped to his feet in amazement and eventually fell to his knees in worship, all because he saw Jesus.

King Nebuchadnezzar sent this message to the people of every race and nation and language throughout the world:

"Peace and prosperity to you!
"I want you all to know about the miraculous signs and wonders the Most High God has performed for me.

How great are his signs,
how powerful his wonders!
His kingdom will last forever,
his rule through all generations."

DANIEL 4:1-3

After Nebuchadnezzar met Jesus, his life was never the same again. In the first three chapters of Daniel, he was an arrogant king obsessed with his greatness. But in chapter 4, he became a man who had been wrecked by a God who loved him enough to reveal Himself through creation, people, circumstances, and Jesus.

With Jesus, we can overcome any situation that comes our way, no matter how out of control things seem or how overwhelmed we may feel.

On a recent trip to Israel, I stood looking at a place believed to be Golgotha, where Jesus was crucified. I thought about how insane that day must have been for those who followed Jesus, how out of control everything must have seemed. How beatings, hammers, nails, and angry crowds pretty much summarized the events of the day. How hopes that had been built over a period of three years were dashed in a six-hour window. And how it must have seemed that either God didn't care about Jesus or God had completely lost control.

However, during that time when it seemed that God was most out of control, we know He was actually in complete control. He used the pain Jesus went through for salvation for us and for the greater good of all humanity. And three days later, Jesus walked away from death—the most overwhelming situation He could have faced.

I still wrestle with anxiety from time to time, especially in situations where I have little control. However, when I think of Jesus, I am reminded that when I feel out of control, God is still in control.

• • •

When we walk through overwhelming situations, we often conclude that either God has forgotten about us or He doesn't care at all.

I've learned during these times that instead of asking God to give me a sign or prove Himself, all I have to do is take a look around at the reminders He has placed in my path that scream that I matter, that I'm important to Him, and that He is way closer than I can imagine. He has given you the same reminders—His creation, the people who demonstrate His love, your circumstances, and Jesus Himself. Overwhelming circumstances often cause us to take our eyes off of the obvious. It's my prayer that we will take a few minutes to focus on the sticky notes that God Himself has given us to demonstrate how much we mean to Him.

CHAPTER 18

STOP IT!

I'm sort of an extreme person (except maybe when it comes to tubing).

When I say I'm going to do something, I try to give it 110 percent. This is especially true in terms of exercise.

When I go to the gym, I'm not there to make friends, get carried away in conversation, or model the latest spandex attire. I am there to try to make my heart explode.

Combine that with the fact that I sweat very easily, and you're probably getting the picture that working out around me can be extremely gross. I've even been asked by a couple of gyms where I've had a membership to please bring towels from home so I could clean up the puddles of sweat around the machine I was working on when I was done.

Beyond the ick factor, my extreme workouts have also resulted in dehydration a time or two. In fact, one time I was so dehydrated that I passed out on the side of a highway while attempting to run a marathon.

So several years ago I began swinging by a nearby gas station after going to the gym with one goal in mind: to pick up a bottle of Gatorade so I could replenish some of the fluids I'd lost. One day, after a particularly grueling workout (meaning my shoes were squishing with sweat when I walked out of the gym), I staggered toward my car and thought, *This is going to be a Gatorade day!*

I purchased the Gatorade and headed back to the car, my feet still squishing, and twisted off the cap. Then I put the drink to my lips, expecting the really cold, refreshing liquid to hit my mouth. I couldn't wait.

But nothing came out!

I looked at the bottle a little puzzled, shook it up really hard (I have no idea why), and then tried to drink again.

And still I got nothing.

At this point I was angry—really angry. I concluded that I'd bought a defective Gatorade and was about to squish my way back inside and demand another one when I had this thought: *Maybe I should remove the cap and see if something is stopping the Gatorade from coming out.*

I will admit that I'm not the sharpest knife in the drawer. You've probably already figured out that, duh, the Gatorade wouldn't come out because of the piece of plastic that needed to be removed from the bottle.

> **Repentance is a change of mind that brings about a change in behavior.**

Sure enough, that one little piece of plastic was stopping me from replenishing what I'd lost. Once I removed it, the Gatorade flowed freely and I was able to be refreshed.

As I sat in my car holding that little piece of plastic, I thought, *If I saw this on the sidewalk or on the floor, it wouldn't seem like a big deal. However, because it was between the refreshing drink and me, it was a very big deal!* I needed Gatorade, but a little piece of plastic was holding me back.

That little piece of plastic had to be removed before I could receive something beneficial.

If you are overwhelmed right now, it's time to face the possibility that one of the reasons you're feeling that way might be because something is blocking your refreshment from the Lord. Maybe there's a barrier that needs to be removed so you can receive the gifts He desires for you.

That barrier is what the Bible refers to as sin.

Now let me say clearly here that when we're feeling overwhelmed, it's not always the result of sin. Sometimes it's simply the result of circumstances beyond our control, not because of anything we've done wrong. But when those anxious feelings come over us, it's a good time to take stock of our lives and see if there's any sin that's hindering us. As Scripture says, "Let us strip off every weight that slows us down, especially the sin that so easily trips us up. And let us run with endurance the race God has set before us" (Hebrews 12:1).

In today's culture, the temptation is to look at sins and refer to them as issues, mistakes, or problems. And as long as we see sin as something that we need to learn to cope with rather than something that needs to be removed, we will never take the action necessary to peel the cap off the bottle so we can be spiritually refreshed.

Sin is a big deal. God still loves us when we sin. It's not His love for us that is in question; it's our love for Him.

If we're not experiencing abundant life, joy, peace, and fulfillment in Him, it's time to pay attention and do a heart examination.

The practice of removing sin from our lives is something that has historically been referred to as repentance. *Repentance* is a word that has negative connotations for many people, especially those of us with a background in church culture. Maybe you've heard a red-faced preacher yelling at the top of his lungs that you need to repent and quit drinking, smoking, cussing, sleeping around, and going to R-rated movies (unless they're about Jesus).

I'm sure those preachers mean well; however, no amount of yelling will bring about true repentance. It's only when we're willing to deal with the heart and not just the behavior that we can really repent. We need to deal with how we think, not just how we behave, so we can get to the root of the problem.

Repentance is a change of mind that brings about a change in behavior. So before we can truly change our behavior, we need to change our minds. And before we can truly change our minds, we must see sin as Jesus sees sin. When we see as He sees, we're much more likely to do what He says.

Ironically, one of the biggest factors that war against true repentance is Christian culture. We know what to say and when to say it, so we try to fake our way through. We show up at church week after week and raise our hands, sing for hours, volunteer, and get goose bumps, but then we go back to our unchanged, unrefreshed lives because we're focused on our external behavior, not our hearts.

This is why some people can attend church for twenty-five years and never change. They are passionate about following the rules while being passive about where they stand with God.

So here's my question for you: Is there anything in your life like that piece of plastic on the Gatorade bottle—something you've been trying to deny rather than deal with?

If so, it's time to face it! But be encouraged: refreshment always follows repentance. Paul puts it this way in his letter to the Corinthian church: "The kind of sorrow God wants us to experience leads us away from sin and results in salvation. There's no regret for that kind of sorrow" (2 Corinthians 7:10).

"Stop Sinning and Do What Is Right"

You'll remember that King Nebuchadnezzar was plagued by a dream in Daniel 2, and now a couple of chapters later, we read about another dream that absolutely freaked him out. I'm not sure if he was making lots of late-night runs to Taco Bell or if he just had a disturbed mind, but this dude had some really whacked-out dreams.

In the dream, the king saw a huge, honkin' tree that got cut down. Nebuchadnezzar was sure someone was trying to say something to him, but he had no idea what—or who—it was.

So, just as he'd done before, he called in his advisers. This time he told them about the dream, but they were just as confused as he was. Then he turned to Daniel, knowing he had a pretty consistent track record with interpreting dreams. After Nebuchadnezzar told Daniel his dream, Daniel's response went something like this: "Uh, you're really not going to like the interpretation of this one!"

Nebuchadnezzar kept pressing him, wanting to know about the dream and specifically about the tree that got cut down. So Daniel finally gave him the 411, saying, "Well, King Neb, you have become proud of your strength and power, and there's some pretty bad stuff going on in your life right now. God has had enough. The tree is you, and God is about to cut you down."

That was definitely *not* what Nebuchadnezzar wanted to hear.

But then Daniel offered him this encouragement: "King Nebuchadnezzar, please accept my advice. Stop sinning and do what is right. Break from your wicked past and be merciful to the poor. Perhaps then you will continue to prosper" (Daniel 4:27).

One of the greatest gifts God can give us is the revelation of our own sinfulness.

He does so not to condemn us but rather to correct us. According to Romans 8:1, "Now there is no condemnation for those who belong to Christ Jesus." And Jesus Himself said that He did not come to condemn the world (see John 3:17). But because God is a loving Father, He wants to correct us. He knows the long-term impact of sin and how it can destroy our lives, and He wants us to be right with Him.

God revealed to Nebuchadnezzar that he was prideful and arrogant, and Daniel begged the king to change his mind, to stop being obsessed with his own greatness.

Unfortunately for the king, he didn't choose the path of repentance.

All these things did happen to King Nebuchadnezzar. Twelve months later he was taking a walk on the flat roof of the royal palace in Babylon. As he looked out across the city, he said, "Look at this great city of Babylon! By my own mighty power, I have built this beautiful city as my royal residence to display my majestic splendor."

While these words were still in his mouth, a voice called down from heaven, "O King Nebuchadnezzar, this message is for you! You are no longer ruler of this kingdom. You will be driven from human society. You will live in the fields with the wild animals, and you will eat grass like a cow. Seven periods of time will pass while you live this way, until you learn that

the Most High rules over the kingdoms of the world and gives
them to anyone he chooses."

That same hour the judgment was fulfilled, and
Nebuchadnezzar was driven from human society. He ate grass
like a cow, and he was drenched with the dew of heaven. He
lived this way until his hair was as long as eagles' feathers and
his nails were like birds' claws.

DANIEL 4:28-33

I'm not going to lie—that's one of the freakiest passages in the Bible.
Sort of like Stephen King meets the Holy Spirit and they write a scary
story.

The Lord brought Nebuchadnezzar down, just like the tree he'd seen
in the dream.

It would be really sad if the story ended here, but it doesn't. If you
aren't dead, then God is not done with you yet. And as long as there is
air in your lungs, you still have an opportunity to turn away from sin
and turn back to the Lord.

Most people, including Nebuchadnezzar himself, must have thought
that his time was over, that God had given up on him. After all, he
went from ruling as a king in a palace
to eating grass like an animal that wasn't
house trained and had to live outside.

**If you aren't dead,
then God is not done
with you yet.**

But then we see that it's not "game
over" for Nebuchadnezzar. Here's what
he says:

After this time had passed, I, Nebuchadnezzar, looked up to
heaven. My sanity returned, and I praised and worshiped the
Most High and honored the one who lives forever.

His rule is everlasting,
    and his kingdom is eternal.

All the people of the earth
    are nothing compared to him.
He does as he pleases
    among the angels of heaven
    and among the people of the earth.
No one can stop him or say to him,
    "What do you mean by doing these things?"

DANIEL 4:34-35

Nebuchadnezzar didn't get restored because he said, "I've got to quit running around, howling at the moon, and peeing on bushes." It wasn't his behavior that was the real problem; it was the way he thought, the way he viewed God and himself.

It's when he repented that his life was restored:

When my sanity returned to me, so did my honor and glory and kingdom. My advisers and nobles sought me out, and I was restored as head of my kingdom, with even greater honor than before.

Now I, Nebuchadnezzar, praise and glorify and honor the King of heaven. All his acts are just and true, and he is able to humble the proud.

DANIEL 4:36-37

Here's the lie we believe: *If I repent of my sin—if I make my sin known and talk about it—God will push me down.*

But the consequences of concealment are far greater than the consequences of confession.

Just because we succeed in hiding our sin from other people doesn't mean we've been successful in hiding our sin from God. He knows all!

Had Nebuchadnezzar repented of his sin and asked for help when he first received the dream from God, he could have avoided seven years of incredibly difficult times. But he didn't, and he faced the consequences.

God isn't trying to push you down; He wants to lift you up.

God isn't trying to hold you back; He's trying to set you free.

God isn't trying to make you feel bad; He's trying to release you from what's making you feel bad.

God brought Nebuchadnezzar to a better place in life because he repented. The end of the chapter records that he praised and glorified God, acknowledging that everything He does is right. Nebuchadnezzar boldly proclaimed, "All his acts are just and true, and he is able to humble the proud" (Daniel 4:37). God had changed Nebuchadnezzar's mind, which put him in a place where he could be refreshed and revived.

If God did this for Nebuchadnezzar thousands of years ago, then why wouldn't He do the same for us? God wants even greater things for us than we want for ourselves. All He asks of us is that we repent.

What's Your One Thing?

The New Testament records a similar story about someone who struggled with pride and the need for repentance. In this account, we see Jesus interact with someone often referred to as "the rich young ruler."

> Once a religious leader asked Jesus this question: "Good Teacher, what should I do to inherit eternal life?"
>
> "Why do you call me good?" Jesus asked him. "Only God is truly good. But to answer your question, you know the commandments: 'You must not commit adultery. You must not murder. You must not steal. You must not testify falsely. Honor your father and mother.'"
>
> The man replied, "I've obeyed all these commandments since I was young."
>
> When Jesus heard his answer, he said, "There is still one thing you haven't done. Sell all your possessions and give the money to the poor, and you will have treasure in heaven. Then come, follow me."

But when the man heard this he became very sad, for he was very rich.

LUKE 18:18-23

In this text we see Jesus deal head-on with the one thing that was holding this guy back.

The rich young ruler was obsessed with his own goodness and tried to emphasize to Jesus how good he was; however, he knew deep down that something was missing in his life. He looked good on the outside, but there was a disconnect happening internally. He couldn't seem to stop focusing on his good behavior instead of his heart.

We often get caught in this trap—keeping our eyes on what we're doing right so we don't have to deal with what's going wrong. And Jesus saw through that right away.

I find it interesting to note Jesus' response to the young man: "There is still one thing you haven't done."

Hold on. Really? *One thing*?

Was the rich young ruler really so amazing that he had only one thing he needed to deal with?

Not likely!

The point isn't that this guy was about as close to perfect as a person could be but rather that Jesus was choosing to deal with the one thing that was competing the most for the rich young ruler's heart.

Jesus didn't overwhelm this guy with a list of things he needed to stop doing in order to be refreshed. Instead, He chose to deal with the one thing that was most messed up in his life.

Unlike Nebuchadnezzar's story, the story of the rich young ruler doesn't have a happy ending. In fact, it seems that this man drifted away into obscurity because he apparently refused to change the way he thought in response to Jesus' challenge.

So what's your "one thing"?

I'm not asking you to make a list of everything you've ever done wrong, every sin you've ever committed. I just want you to consider this simple question: What one thing is standing between you and a closer relationship with Jesus?

We will never overcome our feelings of anxiety and experience times of refreshment until we deal head-on with the sin that is holding us captive. I invite you to join me in the chapters ahead as we look at some of the most common sins that prevent us from the refreshment Christ desires for us.

CHAPTER 19

SIN STRUGGLE #1: SEX

Sex is the one thing everyone thinks about but no one wants to talk about . . . especially in church!

You can find plenty of people in church ranting about "these kids today" who are having inappropriate relationships, but it's rare to find people who engage in honest conversations about sex, because doing so means embracing the uncomfortable. So while the church as a whole has remained silent on this critical topic, Hollywood has seized a megaphone and taught our culture about "values." And we wonder why our society's views on sex and relationships are so messed up!

According to Scripture, God's view of sex is quite simple: before marriage, no sex; get married to someone, and then enjoy sex with that person for the rest of your life. Or as I like to say, "Before marriage, hands off. After marriage, buy some Gatorade, vitamins, and candles and make up for lost time!"

You might be disagreeing with me right now. Maybe you think sex isn't really that big of a deal and that God is restricting your fun by saying no to sex before marriage.

If that's your assumption, there's something important you need to realize: God created sex. He specifically designed males and females to be sexually compatible. (In other words, the parts fit!)

He intended sex to be enjoyed in the context of marriage, not to prevent us from fun but to protect us from the damage sex can cause outside those boundaries.

Some people argue that sex is "just physical" and that Christians make too big of an issue of it. I would simply say that if sex isn't a big deal, then why is it such a big deal in so many songs and movies today?

Why is heartache always involved when the relationship is severed?

If sex is merely physical, then why are people who are sexually abused always devastated?

If sex is only physical, then why do so many people carry around shame and regret from sexual experiences they had many years ago?

Scripture makes it clear that this isn't just a physical issue; it's ultimately a spiritual matter. "Dear brothers and sisters, we urge you in the name of the Lord Jesus to live in a way that pleases God, as we have taught you. You live this way already, and we encourage you to do so even more. For you remember what we taught you by the authority of the Lord Jesus" (1 Thessalonians 4:1-2). It really comes down to a choice: Will we live to please ourselves or the Lord?

If we are followers of Christ, we are called to surrender our obsession with pleasing ourselves. Which is extremely difficult since we are all selfish people.

I remember one time when Lucretia and I were hanging out with some friends, and we all stopped by Bruster's. Lucretia and I decided to split a hot fudge brownie sundae, and honestly I was pretty excited about that idea, because she doesn't eat a lot. I was confident I'd get to eat about 75 percent of the ice cream while she'd eat only a few bites.

Things didn't quite turn out as planned.

Lucretia had worked out hard that day and hadn't eaten much for lunch, so by the time we arrived at Bruster's, she was starving. I was in the middle of a conversation with our friends when I suddenly realized she wasn't saying a whole lot. I discovered why when I looked down at "our" dessert. It was nearly gone!

I wish I could tell you that I responded with complete understanding and compassion, but that would be a lie.

Later that evening I realized that the reason I'd become angry with Lucretia was because I'm selfish. I wanted most of the dessert. I wanted her to have less so I could have more. And when I didn't get what I wanted, I became angry.

Selfishness has a way of clouding our judgment so we can't see what's wrong with us and instead focus on other people's problems.

Sex outside of marriage is a selfish act. It isn't about doing what's right for the other person; it's about satisfying a desire in ourselves. It doesn't come from a heart that genuinely cares for others but rather from a self-centered desire to manipulate them.

A Surefire Way to Kill the Work of God in Your Life

Paul continues in his letter to the Thessalonian church, "God's will is for you to be holy, so stay away from all sexual sin" (1 Thessalonians 4:3).

One of the most frequent questions I have received as a minister over the past twenty years is, "How can I know God's will?" Let me fill you in on a secret: the best way to know God's will is to accept anything the Bible specifically says is His will. This passage is as clear as a "Hot Now" sign at Krispy Kreme: God's will is for us to stay away from sexual sin.

I have a good friend who has a shellfish allergy. It's kind of strange—he didn't develop it until later in life, when he was in college. One night he went to eat shrimp with some friends, and within an hour, his tongue had swelled up to the size of an apple, he had broken out in hives, and he was running around his room thinking he was going to die.

After an eventful trip to the ER and a follow-up appointment with his doctor, he was informed that he should stay away from shellfish, because eating them could kill him.

Needless to say, he doesn't visit all-you-can-eat crab leg buffets at the beach anymore, because he knows it could be deadly for him. He has learned to stay away from something that has the power to kill him.

Sexual sin will kill the work of God in you faster than any other sin.

I've heard people say that every sin is the same and that having sex with someone and stealing a piece of gum at the store are the same in God's eyes. But the Bible says that there are more serious consequences for some sins: "Run from sexual sin! No other sin so clearly affects the body as this one does. For sexual immorality is a sin against your own body" (1 Corinthians 6:18).

Followers of Jesus should be known not just by what we run from but also what we run to. It's a spiritual impossibility to pursue Jesus and sexual immorality at the same time.

Paul charges us to learn self-control: "Then each of you will control his own body and live in holiness and honor—not in lustful passion like the pagans who do not know God and his ways. Never harm or cheat a fellow believer in this matter by violating his wife, for the Lord avenges all such sins, as we have solemnly warned you before" (1 Thessalonians 4:4-6).

> **Followers of Jesus should be known not just by what we run from but also what we run to.**

Given the culture we live in, the call to stay sexually pure can be completely overwhelming.

Before I came to Christ, I had no reason not to do whatever I could with girls, to see how far I could go, to see who I could conquer. After receiving Jesus into my life, my priorities changed . . . but my desires did not quickly follow.

Sexual temptation was something I had to fight nearly every day. When Lucretia and I started dating, I decided at the beginning of our relationship that I was going to fight for our sexual purity rather than surrender to the moments we might find ourselves in.

During this dating period, I spoke about sexual purity at a youth camp. At the end of my talk, a college student came up to me and said, "All that stuff you said about sex was nonsense. You don't know what it's like. Heck, I'll bet you never even struggle with wanting to have sex."

"Dude! I want to have sex all the time," I told him. "In fact, I want to have sex right now. Not with you, though!"

The challenge for me as I pursued Jesus was to lead Lucretia away from the bedroom, not toward it.

A High-Stakes Battleground

In our culture, the battle for purity tends to be somewhat different for men and women.

We'll deal with the men first.

I recently read a statistic that said the porn industry in the United States makes more money than the NFL, the NBA, and Major League Baseball combined every year.[3] In the past two decades, the battle has intensified as porn has become more accessible than ever. You used to have to walk into a shady convenience store to buy it when no one else was looking; today you can simply download it onto your phone.

I battled with an addiction to porn for more than fifteen years—both before and after meeting Jesus. I know firsthand that a man who is trying to follow Christ but who continually jumps back into looking at porn is constantly battling overwhelming shame, guilt, and frustration.

When I was in the eighth grade, my father bought a satellite dish. (This was back when satellite dishes were about the size of actual satellites in space.) It wasn't long before I learned how to channel-surf, and as a fourteen-year-old boy with raging hormones, I quickly discovered the "dirty channels."

This was the gateway into an addiction that ended up dominating my mind and darkening my soul for years after that point.

When I met Christ in 1990, I thought my battle was over. However, a few months later, after the emotional high of getting saved wore off, I found myself drifting into that dangerous territory over and over again. Then, in 1996, when I got Internet access in my apartment, it nearly destroyed me.

You can't have a close, intimate relationship with Jesus and be addicted to porn. Sure, you can know a lot of information about Him, but you won't experience the transformation He wants to bring you—and you won't experience the refreshment He promises in His Word.

Finally, in 1999, I knew it was time to confess my addiction. I was tired of struggling with this sin, and I knew I needed help. James 5:16 says, "Confess your sins to each other and pray for each other so that you may be healed."

Many people receive forgiveness for sin but never experience healing because they choose to conceal rather than to confess. A critical part of the repentance process involves confessing our sins to someone else, which is really tough because it requires us to let go of our pride.

I had a choice to make: Would I let my relationship with Christ be hindered because of my pride, or would I humble myself enough to experience freedom and repentance?

Ultimately I confessed my sin to someone I love and trust. It was one of the toughest things I've ever done, but I have been "porn free" since 1999, and I can tell you that when I rooted that sin out of my life, my walk with God soared to levels I'd never previously experienced.

I know there are women who struggle with pornography too, but for many women, the bigger struggle comes in the realm of compromise. The specifics may look a little different for each person, but this is something that affects single and married women alike.

Married women are often tempted to compromise by starting a relationship that engages them emotionally. And just like with the pornography battle, the easiest place for women to go down this road is on the Internet. Decades ago, it seemed like when a marriage was blown apart by an affair, it was often the man who was messing around. However, times have changed. In my role as a pastor, I have noticed an increase in the number of women leaving their families to pursue relationships outside the bounds of marriage.

The scenario might look something like this. A woman begins to feel unimportant or unnecessary to her husband, so she goes online and begins a conversation with an old flame. It's quite innocent at first—maybe a little flirting, but nothing too serious. However, as time goes by and feelings are shared, an emotional connection starts to form. Soon desires are being expressed and even fulfilled on that slippery path of compromise.

I have seen too many lives torn apart and families shattered by a scenario like this one. This kind of compromise has the power to destroy the work God wants to do in you and through you, so I urge you to fight this battle with everything in you!

If you are a woman who has become locked in emotionally with someone online, I can promise you that the good feelings you hope to experience by connecting with another man will last for only a short time, and a lifetime of pain, regret, and doubt will follow.

If you are struggling with this issue, I encourage you to talk with a friend who knows and loves you and who loves Jesus.

You may even need to take a drastic step, like deleting your Facebook account or changing your e-mail address.

Do whatever it takes to separate you from whatever will kill the work of God in you.

For women who aren't married, the biggest temptation to compromise usually comes in dating decisions.

All too often, single women date guys they should never go out with in the first place. If this is the spot you find yourself in, let me tell you clearly: God has not called you to be a "missionary dater"!

I've seen it happen over and over again: a young woman loves Jesus but begins to hang out with a guy who may give lip service to God but doesn't have an active, ongoing relationship with Him. This guy tags along with her to church and says the right things, and all the while she's banking on the hope that ultimately she'll be able to change him.

And then, as the relationship progresses, she begins to fear she'll be alone if she doesn't give in to him physically, so she allows him to make advances and eventually compromises on her beliefs. She justifies her decision by convincing herself that he loves her and that this will lead to something good. But while compromise may bring temporary satisfaction, it will inevitably clog her connection with Jesus.

Every time I preach a message on God's forgiveness, at least one woman approaches me after the service and asks, "Does God really forgive *every* sin?" And when she shares the rest of her story, I almost always find that she's dealing with the destruction that has been wreaked on her life by sexual sin.

If you are a woman who wrestles with a past marked by unwise and impure decisions, rest in the truth that God knew you and knew every sinful decision you would make before He even created you. He is not surprised by your past. And while you cannot go back and undo what happened, you *can* make the decision to walk more closely with Jesus from this point forward. You can choose not to compromise your morals and convictions from this point forward.

Compromise will promise to be a pathway to freedom, but the opposite is true: it only leads to guilt, frustration, and anxiety.

Living a Holy Life

Purity is not something that comes naturally—for men or women. It's something that must be fought for.

But the battle is worth the fight, because ultimately it isn't just our bodies that are at stake but also our souls: "God has called us to live holy lives, not impure lives. Therefore, anyone who refuses to live by these rules is not disobeying human teaching but is rejecting God, who gives his Holy Spirit to you" (1 Thessalonians 4:7-8).

God doesn't make rules out of cruelty or a power trip, but rather out of love. He has designed us and He has designed sex, so He knows better than anyone else how they work best—according to His good plans.

If sexual sin is the one thing that you need to repent of, I encourage you to do so right now. Take it from someone who fought this battle for years and was consumed with anxiety and guilt because of it: you don't have to keep living this way. You can be free from the overwhelming chains of sexual sin that are keeping you captive. Through confession and repentance, you can overcome what used to own you.

CHAPTER 20

SIN STRUGGLE #2: GREED

Several years ago Lucretia and I were at a friend's house, where I was watching the Lakers play in an NBA play-off game.

Let me tell you, I *love* NBA play-off basketball. The players play hard, the crowds are loud, and the excitement on the court can be felt in practically any living room around the world.

Not only do I love NBA play-off basketball, but I have always been a Lakers fan. So I was excited out of my mind that they were making a great run in the play-offs that particular year.

I timed it so we could leave our friend's house at halftime and be home in time for the beginning of the third quarter. We planned to put together something quick for dinner and eat in the living room so I could watch the game.

While we were on our way home, Lucretia said, "I think I'm just going to have a bowl of cereal for dinner, but I just remembered we don't have any milk. Can you stop by the store and let me run in really quickly to buy some?"

In that instant, I went from NBA bliss to all-out anger. Never mind that I took a vow. Never mind that I'm supposed to love my wife the way Jesus loves the church. Never mind that I'm supposed to put her before me. This was NBA play-off basketball, and I wasn't going to miss it.

So I told her, "No! But I can drive home faster, and when we get there you can take your car and go to the store and get some milk."

Needless to say, there was a strain on our relationship for the rest of the night. I had become obsessed with what I wanted, and it quickly turned into full-fledged greed.

Greed has never helped any relationship, and it always damages our relationship with Jesus. We can't expect to live as overcomers if our lives are bogged down by greed.

What God Has to Say about Greed

Sometimes we fool ourselves into believing that getting what we want or having more of something will satisfy us. But in reality, the opposite is true. Greed actually causes us to be overwhelmed, because when we are greedy, our desire to acquire goes haywire. Our focus becomes what we have (or don't have) rather than who we are in Christ.

Proverbs 15:27 says, "Greed brings grief to the whole family, but those who hate bribes will live." It is so messed up that we would actually believe that having a lot more of what we already have would somehow cause our overwhelmed feelings to go away!

Greed comes in many forms—as a selfish desire for getting our own way, for more attention, for more stuff. But one of the most common ways it rears its head is with money.

Jesus addressed this issue head-on: "No one can serve two masters. For you will hate one and love the other; you will be devoted to one and despise the other. You cannot serve both God and money" (Matthew 6:24).

For many of us, money is the number one competitor for our hearts. It's interesting to note here that Jesus didn't say we can't serve both God and the devil, which is what I would have expected. Instead He said that the opposite of serving God is serving money. The Bible goes so far as to say that "the love of money is the root of all kinds of evil" (1 Timothy 6:10).

One of the stories in the Bible that highlights the destructive power of greed is the account of a man named Achan.

The nation of Israel had been wandering in the desert for forty years (most likely because they were led by a man who refused to stop at a gas station and ask for directions!). They crossed over the Jordan River and were on their way to take possession of the land God had promised them. The first battle they were to fight was the battle of Jericho.

We see God's expectations clearly defined in Joshua 6:18-19: "Do not take any of the things set apart for destruction, or you yourselves will be completely destroyed, and you will bring trouble on the camp of Israel. Everything made from silver, gold, bronze, or iron is sacred to the LORD and must be brought into his treasury."

God was saying that everything in the city belonged to Him—period. Anyone who touched what belonged to Him would be completely destroyed.

Things went quite well for the Israelites in the battle—they whipped rear end and took over the city and then began to plan their next phase of attack. However, someone ignored God's instructions about not bringing home loot. As a result, the next time the Israelites went out to fight, they came back to camp with their tails between their legs. As we say in the South, they'd been "whupped real bad"!

> **When we are greedy, our desire to acquire goes haywire.**

They began to try to figure out what had happened—why they'd been overwhelmed by the enemy. Finally, after some digging around, they discovered what Achan had done.

Here is his confession: "It is true! I have sinned against the LORD, the God of Israel. Among the plunder I saw a beautiful robe from Babylon, 200 silver coins, and a bar of gold weighing more than a pound. I wanted them so much that I took them. They are hidden in the ground beneath my tent, with the silver buried deeper than the rest" (Joshua 7:20-21).

Needs vs. Wants

Achan lived thousands of years ago, but there's plenty we can learn from his story. We're going to break down three key phrases in his confession that I think all of us can relate to.

I Saw

"Among the plunder *I saw* . . ." (Joshua 7:21, emphasis added).

I'm not sure if I'm alone in this, but I absolutely detest infomercials. I can be flipping the channels on my TV and land on one, and within thirty seconds I'm hooked. Up until that moment, I'd been completely unaware of that product's existence. And now suddenly my life feels incomplete without it.

The world has quite a knack for showing us things we "need."

We walk through the mall completely satisfied with the clothes in our closet . . . until we see the latest style in the window of our favorite store.

We love our TV . . . until we go to our neighbors' house and see their brand-new, state-of-the-art surround-sound home theater system.

We are happy with the car we drive . . . until our best friend pulls up in his fully loaded, leather-interior, new-smelling ride.

We like our shoes . . . until we see a friend who has a pair that would go perfectly with an outfit we have in our closet.

When we see things we don't need but something or someone tries to convince us would make our lives better, we start to go down that slippery slope toward greed.

I Wanted

"*I wanted* them so much . . ." (Joshua 7:21, emphasis added).

If we stare at something long enough, it can become an intense desire.

All of us want things we don't need or can't have. Far too many young people are up to their eyeballs in debt because they wanted to live the same lifestyle as their parents, not comprehending that it took their parents years to get there.

Wanting something is not a sin.

However, if wanting something leads us to compromise what God's Word clearly says about money, that's always a sin.

A few years ago I started a new diet, and my main goal was to stay away from sweets. I was convinced that if I cut out sweets, I'd be able to take off about ten pounds. So that first Monday of my healthy eating plan, I rolled out of bed early and went to the gym, taking my workout intensity up a notch to prove I was serious about my weight-loss goals.

A few minutes after I began my workout, a woman who attends our church walked up to me with something really big wrapped in aluminum foil.

"Perry, I was hoping I would see you here," she said. "Last night I made my famous chocolate cake. It's seriously the best thing you will ever put in your mouth, and I knew you'd want a piece."

You have got to be kidding, I thought. *Dessert at the gym? Well, I'm not going to eat it. I'll be nice and take it home, but when I get it there, I'm going to throw it away.*

I finished my workout, grabbed the cake, and went home. I walked straight to the kitchen, fully intending to throw the whole thing away, but before I did, I thought, *I should at least see what it looks like.*

I unwrapped it, and food lust immediately overwhelmed me. It was the prettiest piece of chocolate cake I'd ever seen. Seven layers, all perfectly even, with lots and lots of icing.

That's when the smell hit me and I lost all sense of self-control.

I Took

"I wanted them so much that *I took* them" (Joshua 7:21, emphasis added).

By the time Lucretia found me in the kitchen, I had completely devoured the cake and was literally licking the aluminum foil to make sure I didn't miss any chocolate.

Greed causes us to take what we don't need and can't afford. It tempts us to arrange our finances so they serve our wants, not what God wants.

And greed always leads us to make really dumb decisions.

I once had a car that was a really good car. It drove well and never had any mechanical issues. My plan was to drive it for quite a while . . . until I saw the red SUV on sale at a local car dealership.

I saw it, so I stopped and looked at it. The more I looked at it, the more I wanted it. After test-driving it, I made the arrangements to take it. I signed a note to finance a four-year-old car for 84 months at 12 percent interest.

Unfortunately, that's a true story. That's where my greed landed me. It's not wrong to want nice things or even to have nice things. But it is wrong when nice things *have you*. When we find ourselves starting to rationalize or ignore what the Bible says about money, it's time to do a serious reevaluation of our actions and the motives behind them.

The Destructive Path of Greed

Greed has more power to destroy the work of God inside us than we can fathom.

For one thing, greed often leads to debt. Sometimes debt is the result of an unexpected illness, a lost job, or unforeseen expenses, but in many cases debt comes as a result of buying things we don't need with money we don't have to try to impress people we don't really like. It's hard to serve Jesus if we're serving people who sold us stuff we couldn't afford.

Scripture makes it clear that debt can be one of the most overwhelming situations on the planet. "Just as the rich rule the poor, so the borrower is servant to the lender" (Proverbs 22:7).

Let's take a look at the outcome of Achan's story:

> Joshua and all the Israelites took Achan, the silver, the robe, the bar of gold, his sons, daughters, cattle, donkeys, sheep, goats, tent, and everything he had, and they brought them to the valley of Achor. Then Joshua said to Achan, "Why have you brought trouble on us? The LORD will now bring trouble on you." And all the Israelites stoned Achan and his family and burned their bodies. They piled a great heap of stones over Achan, which remains to this day. That is why the place has been called the Valley of Trouble ever since. So the LORD was no longer angry.
>
> JOSHUA 7:24-26

Greed always destroys. Achan didn't just lose his own life, but his entire family was also destroyed because he didn't follow what God had made so clear.

I've experienced firsthand the destructive power of greed. When Lucretia and I got married in 2000, we had a combined debt of more than $120,000. Most of it was mine—a combination of credit card debt, student loans, and loans from finance companies. I simply hadn't followed what God's Word says about money. God wasn't first in this area of my life . . . and when He isn't in control of a particular area of our lives, that area is sure to be out of control.

The Bible says, "In him all things hold together" (Colossians 1:17, NIV). So if something is falling apart, it's because it's not in Him.

I had to repent of this area of sin in my life, which meant I had to change my mind about the way I handled money. I made the decision to put God first in my finances and to manage my money God's way from that point on.

Within five years, Lucretia and I were completely debt free, and we've remained that way ever since. It wasn't easy, but the peace that came with being released from debt was worth the effort.

If you are feeling overwhelmed by greed right now, I want to encourage you that there is hope; there is a way out. You don't have to follow in the footsteps of Achan and remain stuck in the cycle of "I saw," "I wanted," "I took." Change begins with a change of mind—choosing to believe that God has already given us everything we truly need.

It's hard to live in a culture that markets to us on a daily basis, telling us that we're incomplete and that what we currently have is not enough. However, if we choose not to buy the lie that more always equals better, we can conquer greed and escape the crushing mountains of worry that come with the territory of debt and foolish financial decisions.

The way to get out of debt isn't just by praying about it; we also need to acknowledge that we have a problem and then be willing to roll up our sleeves and do something about it. It won't be easy, but it will lead to a much more fulfilling life than being stuck in financially overwhelming situations that come when we sit around and do nothing.

CHAPTER 21

SIN STRUGGLE #3: UNFORGIVENESS

Several years ago I bought a brand-new car. I had never owned a new vehicle before, and I eagerly saved money and then made the purchase. It was a black GMC Yukon, and it was one of my favorite things on the entire planet.

One afternoon I had a meeting at a Chick-fil-A restaurant, and after sitting inside sipping sweet tea and talking through some plans for about an hour, I headed outside . . . where I saw one of the absolute worst sights in my life.

Someone had hit my car! My brand-new car! And it wasn't just a scratch—the back left fender was crushed. In fact, a piece of the bumper from the car that had hit my Yukon was lying next to my car.

No problem, I thought, trying to reason through this logically. *The person who did this obviously knows they did it. They probably put a note on my windshield giving me their phone number and telling me to call so we can make financial arrangements to take care of this.*

Wrong!

There was no note. Just a smashed car.

I was angry. So angry that my entire face got hot, my heart rate became elevated, and I began sweating profusely.

I've met well-meaning Christians who have told me I should have stopped and prayed for the person who did that to my car. Actually, I did. I prayed what David prayed in Psalm 3:7—that God would shatter the teeth of the wicked!

As much as I tried, I couldn't get over my anger and unforgiveness. The next morning I woke up and got ready for work and had all but forgotten the incident. But the moment I walked out to my car and saw the damage, I went into outrage mode again.

This went on for about a month. Every time I saw the car, I was robbed of my joy. Finally I began to realize that getting mad was doing me zero good and that I needed to get past this if I was going to enjoy life again.

Maybe significant damage has been done to you—something far worse than a fender bender.

Someone did something wrong.

It hurt then.

It still hurts.

And you can't seem to move past it or get over it.

I've met some people who believe anger and bitterness are just part of life. Some would even go as far as to argue that it's a right. However, when we refuse to forgive and we allow bitterness to reside in our heart, it always interferes with our relationship with God. Unforgiveness holds us back from doing what we've been called to do and becoming who we're called to be.

A Dreamer's Tale of Forgiveness

One of the most amazing stories of forgiveness is the account of Joseph in the Old Testament.

In Genesis 37, we see Joseph as a young, ambitious dreamer who informed his brothers that one day he would rule over them. Combine this with the fact that he was his father's favorite (demonstrated by the coat of many colors his daddy gave him) and the fact that he made it a habit to tell his dad when his brothers got out of line, and you have a recipe for a really great episode of *Jerry Springer*.

One day Joseph's brothers got tired of it all. They tore off his robe, beat him up, and threw him in a pit with the intention of killing him. However, when they discovered they could make some money off him, they sold him to some slave traders.

Joseph was then taken to Egypt, where he was sold into slavery to a guy named Potiphar. Things went well for a while, but then as a result of an unfortunate situation that wasn't his fault, Joseph was thrown into prison and remained there for several years.

Uh, do you think he had any issues with his brothers at that point?

Do you think he remembered the time they beat him up?

Do you think he held something against them for selling him into slavery?

I'm not sure about you, but I want revenge when someone cuts in front of me in line at Starbucks, so I can't imagine how Joey was feeling at this point. I know I would have allowed my mind to go down this path: *One of these days, if I ever get out of here, I'm going to find them and* . . . You can probably fill in the rest.

A funny thing happened, though. Through a set of God-led circumstances, Joseph made it out of prison and was actually put as second-in-command over the entire nation of Egypt. Talk about an intense power swing—he went from prison to the palace and was now in a position to exact revenge on anyone who had hurt him.

And this is where the story gets even crazier.

The entire region was facing a severe famine at the time. Joseph's brothers (along with his father) lived in Israel, and Egypt was the only place that had food for sale—mainly because of Joseph's master economic plan.

So Joseph's brothers came to Egypt, desperately hoping to buy some grain (see Genesis 42). As "luck" would have it, Joseph was the guy people appeared in front of if they wanted to buy food. When his brothers approached him, he knew immediately who they were. They didn't recognize him, however, and they bowed down before him.

Honestly, at this point I would be whipping some rear end. I'd be calling in guards. I'd be calling these guys names. I'd be doing everything I could to even the score.

But Joseph remained calm. He didn't respond in anger or vengeance toward his family. In fact, he didn't even tell his brothers who he was until much later (see Genesis 45:1-8).

I believe he was able to respond this way because he knew that the power of forgiveness was greater than the pain of his circumstances. If he had held on to bitterness and unforgiveness, he wouldn't have been able to accomplish all he did as a leader in his new country.

When we are unwilling to forgive, we become obsessed with our agenda and neglect God's plans altogether.

Joseph, however, refused to allow unforgiveness to overwhelm his life. But even when he extended forgiveness to his brothers, they weren't quite sure if they could buy it (I'm not sure I would have either). Much later, after the death of their father, the brothers became convinced that Joseph was going to lower the boom on them.

After burying Jacob, Joseph returned to Egypt with his brothers and all who had accompanied him to his father's burial. But now that their father was dead, Joseph's brothers became fearful. "Now Joseph will show his anger and pay us back for all the wrong we did to him," they said.

So they sent this message to Joseph: "Before your father died, he instructed us to say to you: 'Please forgive your brothers for the great wrong they did to you—for their sin in treating you so cruelly.' So we, the servants of the God of your father, beg you to forgive our sin." When Joseph received the message, he broke down and wept. Then his brothers came and threw themselves down before Joseph. "Look, we are your slaves!" they said.

But Joseph replied, "Don't be afraid of me. Am I God, that I can punish you? You intended to harm me, but God intended it all for good. He brought me to this position so I could save the lives of many people. No, don't be afraid. I will continue to take care of you and your children." So he reassured them by speaking kindly to them.

GENESIS 50:14-21

This is one of the first times in the Bible the word *forgive* is used. Again we see Joseph assuring the brothers that he had completely forgiven them. And even beyond tolerating his difficult circumstances, he came to a point of believing that "God intended it all for good."

The Real Victim of Unforgiveness

If I'm being perfectly honest here, I have to admit there are certain rules I think should pertain to some people but not necessarily to me.

For example, I think the speed limit is a good idea for most people. After all, those people aren't as good drivers as I am. I'm careful and cautious and can handle my speed.

I think that when you go to the grocery store and push your groceries out in a cart, you should have to return your cart to the return area before you leave. However, I don't think that should always apply to me, as sometimes I'm in a hurry and just don't have the time.

When it comes to forgiveness, most of us feel the same way. We think that if we've done someone wrong or hurt them in some way, we should be forgiven. After all, either we didn't mean to or we just made a bad decision.

All of us want forgiveness, but all too often we refuse to offer to others what we want for ourselves. And in doing so, we limit our intimacy with God. Jesus put it this way: "Forgive others, and you will be forgiven" (Luke 6:37).

Years ago I bought an ab roller, all because of a stupid infomercial. I've always had a flabalanche around my midsection and have wanted to tighten it up. So one night I was flipping the channels, and I saw this amazing product that promised me washboard abs as long as I do it for seven minutes a day.

Seven minutes a day, I thought. *I can do that!*

So I ordered it, set it up in my living room, and began training with such intensity that I just knew it wouldn't be long before I could wash my shirt on my stomach.

I'm sure you will be shocked to hear that it didn't work. I'd put all my hope in the ab roller, and my belly was still in bad shape.

The commercial for the ab roller overpromised and underdelivered. Unforgiveness does the same thing.

Withholding forgiveness does not hurt "them"; it hurts you.

Withholding forgiveness is like drinking poison and expecting it to kill the person who hurt you.

Withholding forgiveness puts a barrier between you and the blessings of God.

Withholding forgiveness overwhelms you with feelings that the human body was not designed to sustain.

I don't know what your specific hurt is, but I imagine the pain runs deep.

Maybe someone raped you or molested you.

Maybe someone stole money from you.

Maybe someone betrayed you.

Maybe someone spread stories about you that weren't true.

And the pain just won't go away.

But for those of us who are followers of Jesus, forgiveness isn't just a good idea; it's something Jesus commanded. And it's not just something Jesus commanded; it's also something He Himself demonstrated.

Being Released from the Prison of Unforgiveness

You know the story—Jesus was betrayed, arrested, beaten, mocked, flogged, and then taken to be crucified.

Talk about a bad day. That makes my damaged car look like a walk in the park.

After all this had been done to Him, Jesus said, "Father, forgive them, for they don't know what they are doing" (Luke 23:34).

One of the most incredible parts of all is that the people who were murdering Him never even asked for forgiveness; He just gave it to them.

I've had people tell me they would forgive someone if the person who offended them apologized and then asked to be forgiven. That's nice when it happens, but the example that has been set before us is to give forgiveness freely—even to those who don't deserve it. Ephesians 4:32 says, "Be kind to each other, tenderhearted, forgiving one another, just as God through Christ has forgiven you."

Forgiving as Christ forgave means forgiving completely and consistently, knowing that Christ forgave us when we didn't deserve it.

What good has ever come from bitterness and unforgiveness?

I can answer this one for all of us. None! It makes us bitter spouses, parents, friends, and coworkers. Forgiveness is like putting a key in a prison door to release someone else, only to discover that the person you are releasing is yourself.

> **Forgiveness is like putting a key in a prison door to release someone else, only to discover that the person you are releasing is yourself.**

• • •

Your particular struggle might not be with sexual sin, greed, or unforgiveness. There's an endless list of sins that can separate us from experiencing God's love and leave us feeling guilty, frustrated, and overwhelmed.

But I'd like to encourage you right now to take a moment to identify that one thing that's holding you back in your walk with God. What one thing should you be fleeing from rather than flirting with?

God wants to remove it from your life, not to make you miserable but rather to prevent misery and shame from coming into your life. He wants to remove whatever will eventually destroy you if you don't walk away.

Don't be afraid to let go of what God is trying to remove. Anytime He asks us to give up something, it's because He wants to give us something even better.

CHAPTER 22

TRUST

In case you haven't figured this out yet, I'm a dad who absolutely adores his little girl.

Last summer while my family was on vacation, Charisse and I were playing in the pool. At one point she got out and stood on the edge for a second, laughing and looking at me.

I held my arms out to her and said, "Jump!"

She shook her head. "No way!"

I was a bit bothered by her refusal to jump; after all, I'm her father. I want nothing but the absolute best for her. I had every intention of making sure no harm came to her. I just wanted her to experience the thrill of being in the air and the safety of being caught by arms that had been catching her all her life.

Again I asked her to jump. She shook her head again, and this time she took a few steps back.

I asked if she was scared, and she let out a very soft, "Yes, sir!"

I swam to the side of the pool, called her over to me, and spoke quietly and directly to her. "Charisse, I am your daddy," I said. "I would never ask you to do anything that would hurt you. I want the best for you, and I promise that if you jump, I'll catch you."

We locked eyes for a second, and I could see there was an internal struggle going on. She wanted to trust me, but I was asking her to do something she'd never done before.

I finally convinced her to jump—and I did manage to catch her. She shrieked and giggled and wanted to do it again . . . and again . . . and again. (I can't remember the last time I went to bed so sore!)

When I reflected on what had happened at the pool that day, I thought, *Children will do anything their father asks them to do if they trust him.*

The same is true of our relationship with our heavenly Father. We will do whatever He asks of us if we truly believe His arms will catch us when we jump.

We live in a skeptical society, and I am one of those skeptics. Many of us find it difficult to trust other people—not just when it comes to jumping into a pool, but in any area of our lives.

> **God wants us to trust Him—not just with the big, eternal things, but with everything.**

In some cases, there's good reason for our skepticism. A company releases a product, does a thirty-minute infomercial about it, and promises that if you buy it, you will lose weight, make more money, and have smoother skin. So you purchase the product, but it doesn't do what the advertisement promised. And a skeptic is born.

Or maybe a friend approaches you and says he'd love to have lunch and tell you about an "amazing opportunity" for your life. You get excited and set up the meeting . . . only to discover that the amazing opportunity begins with your giving him lots and lots of money. Another skeptic is born.

We all have a hard time trusting other people and products, mainly because we've been hurt or lied to in the past, and our natural defense mechanism is to simply not trust anyone. And if we're being completely honest here, we have a difficult time trusting God, too.

We trust Him with things like eternity.

We trust Him to make sure the earth keeps spinning around at the right pace every day.

We trust Him with the oxygen levels in the atmosphere.

But when it comes to trusting Him with every issue in our lives, we have a more difficult time.

The more we hold back from Him, the more we put our trust in ourselves instead of God, the more anxiety we feel.

God wants us to trust Him—not just with the big, eternal things, but with everything. He isn't looking for partial surrender; He wants our total surrender.

In the next two chapters, I offer two reasons why we have a difficult time trusting God and explain how we can move past these trust blockers that hold us back.

CHAPTER 23

TRUST STRUGGLE #1: THE PACE OF OUR LIVES

The story of Jesus' time on earth is found in four accounts in the New Testament—the four Gospels. These books tell about His ministry, which started when He was about thirty years old and lasted three years. He had what we would call rock-star status, as thousands of people followed Him wherever He went. He had so much popularity, in fact, that at times Jesus actively sought to get away from the crowds and take a break.

During the last week of His life, Jesus arrived in Jerusalem. When people saw Him, they started losing their minds—screaming at the top of their lungs, throwing palm branches in front of Him, and shouting "Hosanna!" (which means "please save" or "save now").

His Facebook friends and Twitter followers were *exploding*.

However, in less than a week, things suddenly took a really bad turn. The religious leaders drummed up some false charges against Jesus. They put Him through a joke of a trial. They turned the crowd against Him. Then they turned Him over to the Romans, who beat, mocked, and eventually murdered Him.

It's important to note at this point that a lot of our worry and anxiety come from our obsession over what other people think about us. The story of Jesus Himself makes it clear, however, that those who deify will also crucify. The same people who shouted "Hosanna!" at the beginning of the week also shouted "Crucify!" by the end of that same week.

It's a dangerous thing to place our emotional stability in the hands of people.

It's a dangerous thing to allow those who know us the least to define us the most.

It's a dangerous thing to believe what others say about us rather than what God says about us.

And leaning in to what others say over what God says always raises our level of stress and anxiety.

In Luke's account of Jesus' life, we're told that after Jesus' crucifixion and burial, some women were on their way to the tomb to prepare His body for burial. When they arrived there, though, they discovered that the stone had been rolled away. They were shocked to discover two angels at the tomb, who told them that Jesus wasn't in the grave—that He'd risen, just as He'd said He would. Then the angels told the women to go and tell the disciples.

Definitely *not* what they'd been expecting.

When Peter, one of the disciples in Jesus' inner circle, heard what the women had declared, he took off for the tomb in a sprint. Sure enough, he found that Jesus' body wasn't there . . . but he didn't believe Jesus had actually risen from the dead.

Those who deify will also crucify.

One of the misconceptions we often have about Jesus is that it was just Him and twelve guys (the apostles) who ran around all over Israel together. However, Scripture indicates that Jesus had a larger group of around seventy people who followed Him, and some have even argued that He could have had as many as 120 followers on a pretty consistent basis.

This is important because we assume that the women went back and told just the Twelve about the resurrection. But in reality, they shared the news with a much larger group. Scripture puts it this way: "They rushed back from the tomb to tell his eleven disciples—and everyone else—what had happened" (Luke 24:9).

Scripture tells us what happened next: "That same day two of Jesus' followers were walking to the village of Emmaus, seven miles from Jerusalem" (Luke 24:13).

Before we move on with this story, it's important to note the opening phrase of this verse. It's essential for us to understand that "that same day" means the same day as the Resurrection.

The two followers mentioned in this passage were probably people who had been with Jesus a majority of the time He'd been in ministry. They'd heard Him teach, seen His miracles, and experienced Him on a level we can only dream about.

Next we need to note that these two followers were walking to Emmaus, away from Jerusalem.

What had taken place in Jerusalem? The resurrection! Jerusalem was where the angels had first proclaimed this good news. It was the hub of the most important miracle in human history.

But here we see that two of Jesus' disciples were walking away from the site of the resurrection and toward a village called Emmaus. In other words, these men seemed to be giving up on following Jesus and were now going back to their old lives.

Now I want to emphasize that these guys weren't bad people; they weren't living in some kind of gut-wrenching sin. They just got to a point where it looked like it was game over and they couldn't trust Jesus any longer.

And I have to say, who could blame them? After all, they'd seen Jesus die one of the most gruesome deaths known to humankind. People might come back after a beating, but coming back from the dead was an impossibility.

We often look at the Bible and wonder why people did what they did without realizing that we have the benefit of knowing the end of the story.

Do you really think you would have believed the whole angel-and-resurrection story from some women who seemed completely freaked out? I personally would have thought they must have had a beer or twelve!

For them and for us, it is difficult to believe what we can't perceive. And because of this, we tend to walk away from the very one we should be walking with.

The Danger of Drifting

Drifting is a natural process—and a dangerous one.

In high school I had a friend who went out on a lake, fell asleep on a solar float, and drifted out to the middle of the lake, where he snoozed for more than two hours. He woke up looking like a lobster, and the pain he experienced for the next week or so was nearly unbearable to watch.

If we're not careful, any of us can drift away from Jesus.

Let me ask you a question. Has there ever been a time when you were closer to Jesus than you are right now?

If so, then you have most likely drifted.

I'm not saying you're a bad person.

I'm not about to "lower the boom" on you and give you a good old-fashioned "You're going to hell" sermon.

In fact, I would argue that most people who drift away don't intend to do so. I've never met anyone who told me, "One day I woke up and decided that this was going to be the day I walked away from Jesus."

But every person I know who has followed Christ (and who has been honest with me) has admitted that at some point in their lives they have drifted.

We drift when we submit ourselves to the opinions of others, when we choose to believe what we can see over what we can't, or when we seek to have more control. Every mistake I deeply regret has taken place when I was walking away from Jesus.

Drifting occurs when we know information about Jesus but have no intimacy with Him.

The two people in this story had received information about the Resurrection, but their hearts had not experienced transformation.

They chose to take matters into their own hands and walk the other direction because they just weren't sure they could believe anymore.

The next verse says, "As they walked along they were talking about everything that had happened" (Luke 24:14). Don't miss this—it's possible to have conversations about Jesus while walking away from Him. Just because we talk about Him doesn't mean we have a connection with Him.

However, here is one of the many things I absolutely love about Jesus: anytime we walk away from Him, anytime we drift away, He always comes after us.

And He comes after us not with the purpose of getting back at us but rather with the purpose of bringing us back so we can have fellowship with Him and other people.

Jesus is not full of wrath, hatred, and anger toward us; He is full of grace and mercy. The Bible says that it's His kindness that leads us to turn away from our sin and surrender our lives to Him (see Romans 2:4).

Every time I've drifted away from Jesus, He has loved me enough to pursue me for the purpose of bringing me back.

Every time I've wanted to give up on Him, He has refused to give up on me.

And that's true for you as well.

Watch what happens next: "As they talked and discussed these things, Jesus himself suddenly came and began walking with them" (Luke 24:15). Jesus Himself comes after us when we refuse to believe and try to seize control of our own lives.

Then the Bible says, "But God kept them from recognizing him" (Luke 24:16).

This was the same Jesus they'd been with, listened to, spoken with, and seen perform miracles for the past three years. And yet when He walked alongside them, they didn't recognize Him.

Sometimes we also miss seeing Jesus. It may be because we aren't expecting to see Him or because we are too busy to look for Him.

The Danger of Busyness

On my second trip to Israel, I met someone who has to be one of the coolest people on the planet. He is a Messianic Jewish man named Arie.

He and I were talking about this story, and he told me that one of the things many people miss when they read it is that men from this region of the world are known to be unusually fast walkers.

I know this is not a lie, because the first time we had Arie as a guide, I just about passed out from trying to sustain the pace he was setting. He walked faster than I could jog!

Consider the fact that this was a seven-mile journey. These men were on a mission to get from point A to point B, and a walk like this would have taken a significant amount of time.

And they were having a conversation.

It's nearly impossible to pay attention to anyone or anything around you when you're in a hurry to get somewhere and having a conversation with someone at the same time. Have you ever gotten so caught up in a conversation that you didn't realize what was going on around you? Or have you ever been texting someone and been so involved in the back-and-forth that you weren't aware of the people right in front of you?

One day I had to go to the hospital for a blood test. I pulled into the parking lot and heard one of my friends giving an interview on the radio. I was running late and needed to get inside as quickly as possible to be on time, but my friend was doing such a great job on the interview that I wanted to hear all of it.

After the interview was over, I leaped out of the car and began walking as fast as I could while at the same time texting him to tell him what a great job he'd done.

Bam!

I never saw the tree.

I wound up with a cut on my nose, a bruise on my forehead, and a slightly damaged reputation, simply because I wasn't paying attention to what was going on around me.

Going back to those guys on the road to Emmaus, I think they might have even seen Jesus as an interruption to what they were doing and where they were going. After all, they were on a mission—they had something they needed to accomplish. They were *busy*.

I'm guessing that whoever you are and whatever your stage in life, you'd describe yourself as a busy person. I've never met anyone who told me their biggest problem was to figure out how to use up all their extra time. We all have meetings, lunches, dinners, sporting events, and unplanned emergencies that inconveniently refuse to fit into our calendars.

The devil doesn't want to make you bad; he wants to make you busy. Because if he can make you busy, then eventually he can make you bad.

Busyness always keeps us from recognizing Jesus.

I've had many people tell me, "My schedule is killing me." This took me over a decade to discover, but here's a newsflash: *You are the one who controls your schedule!* And just because you have an opportunity to do something, that doesn't mean you should feel the obligation to do it.

> **The devil doesn't want to make you bad; he wants to make you busy.**

I wrote a lot about rest in chapter 8, so I won't rehash that here except to emphasize that the command that God explained in greatest detail in the Ten Commandments was the one to take a day off!

We will never follow Jesus closely until we see Him clearly, and we can't see Him clearly if we are constantly coming up with to-do lists that are as long as a five-year-old's Christmas list and then frantically trying to scratch off every item by the end of the day—just so we can feel some sense of accomplishment.

The two men on the road to Emmaus were so rushed and so focused on their agenda that they couldn't see the miracle right in front of them. We can learn from them that slowing down isn't just a good idea; it's necessary for us to realize that hope is not lost.

CHAPTER 24

TRUST STRUGGLE #2: DISAPPOINTMENT

Have you ever been disappointed in someone or something?

The answer for all of us is "Yes!" We get our hopes up, only to be let down.

Lucretia and I celebrated our fifth wedding anniversary in Hawaii. When she was a child, her dream was to be a contestant on *The Price Is Right* and win a trip to Hawaii, because she thought that was the only way she'd ever be able to go. However, through careful budgeting and planning, we were able to save enough to make the trip happen. As soon as we arrived, we set out to have the time of our lives.

Now I should tell you here that one of the things I love most about vacation is food.

Whenever I arrive at a place I've never been, I ask the people at the hotel about the best places to eat. As soon as we got to Hawaii, we started hearing that we had to eat at a restaurant at the Four Seasons. It's important to note that we were not staying at the Four Seasons—we were on a budget, so we were staying at what was more like the "One Season."

This restaurant was owned by a guy I'd never heard of named Wolfgang Puck. The first time I heard his name, I thought he was a hockey player, not a chef. People raved about this restaurant so much that I was almost convinced it would be a sin to leave Hawaii and not eat at this place.

So we made reservations and showed up for our much-anticipated meal . . . and it turned out to be one of the top-five most disappointing moments of my life.

Something else you need to know about me, besides that I love food, is that I'm a Southern boy. I like restaurants that put more food onto your plate than you can eat and don't charge you an arm and a leg for it. I like good old "meat and three" restaurants, which are very common in the South. (A meat and three is a place where you get one meat and three vegetables—and there are always biscuits to go along with your meal.)

In a typical meat and three restaurant, you can have a complete meal, including a huge glass of sweet tea, for seven bucks.

There was *nothing* on Mr. Puck's menu for seven dollars.

Not a salad.

Not an appetizer.

Nothing!

"Honey, this is not good," I told Lucretia. "I'm not used to eating in places like this. It's way too fancy for me. I think we need to leave."

She calmed me down and told me to just look at the menu and find something to order. We were in Hawaii, and we didn't know when or if we'd ever have a chance to come back.

So I ordered steak and potatoes—even a fancy restaurant can't mess that up, right?

Wrong!

When they brought me my steak, it couldn't have been much larger than four ounces. I know that some people would consider that a meal; I consider it a snack. I politely asked what had happened to the rest of my steak, and our waiter did not find my comment amusing.

The steak-snack came with what seemed to be a melon scooper–sized portion of mashed potatoes and a whopping two pieces of asparagus.

I completed the meal in about four bites total, and I was very angry with Wolfgang Puck!

After we finished, the waiter came to our table and asked if we wanted dessert.

I always want dessert—always! However, I had been so disappointed with the portion sizes that I was just about to say no when the waiter said, "Our feature dessert special tonight has three scoops of ice cream. . . ."

I didn't hear a thing he said after the "three scoops of ice cream" comment. I love ice cream. I didn't really care if the three scoops of ice cream were on an old shoe—I wanted that dessert. *Maybe,* I thought, *this dessert will make up for the snack they tried to pass off as a meal.*

I sat there dreaming about lots and lots of ice cream entering my mouth and the joy that would be exploding out of me. Three scoops of ice cream—wow, this was going to be a dessert to remember!

And it definitely was.

The dessert had three of the tiniest melon scoops of ice cream I'd ever seen.

Wolfgang Puck had officially become "Wolfgang Suck" in my mind.

"I'm about to turn this place out!" I told Lucretia, with smoke coming out my nose.

"You'd better calm down!"

"In the Bible, when Jesus saw people getting robbed in the Temple, He made a whip and whipped some tail," I responded.

"Well, you're not Jesus," she said. "You're not in Jerusalem, and this is not the Temple. Control yourself!"

Needless to say, as we left that night and walked back to the One Season, I was both disappointed and angry. I had been told I was about to have a great meal, and it turned out to be terrible (by my standards, anyway). I thought my experience was going to go one way, and it wound up taking a turn I hadn't seen coming.

That's my Hawaii story, but for you, that may be your God story.

You thought He was going to do something great, and instead it seemed as if He did nothing at all.

You thought He was going to heal someone close to you, and He didn't.

You thought He was going to give you an amazing job, but you were passed over for the position.

You thought He would have brought a spouse into your life by now, but you're still single and wondering if you'll ever get married.

You thought you and your spouse would have children by now, but things aren't working out as planned.

When we walk through difficult times, it's natural for us to become angry with God and then conclude that because He didn't come through for us, we shouldn't give Him our complete trust.

We have a hard time trusting God because we take our preferences and turn them into His promises—even when those aren't actually things He has promised to do.

Hoping for the Right Thing

Let's go back to the story about the men on the road to Emmaus and notice the conversation that takes place.

> [Jesus] asked them, "What are you discussing so intently as you walk along?"
>
> They stopped short, sadness written across their faces. Then one of them, Cleopas, replied, "You must be the only person in Jerusalem who hasn't heard about all the things that have happened there the last few days."
>
> "What things?" Jesus asked.
>
> "The things that happened to Jesus, the man from Nazareth," they said. "He was a prophet who did powerful miracles, and he was a mighty teacher in the eyes of God and all the people. But our leading priests and other religious leaders handed him over to be condemned to death, and they crucified him. *We had hoped* he was the Messiah who had come to rescue Israel. This all happened three days ago."
>
> LUKE 24:17-21, EMPHASIS ADDED

Notice the emphasized phrase, "we had hoped." Those three words have enormous implications for this story—and for our lives.

Basically they were saying, "We had high hopes for Jesus. We had some personal preferences we felt He should have addressed." And when

Jesus didn't fulfill their expectations, they somehow believed He'd broken a promise and, as a result, couldn't be trusted.

Let me explain the cultural context a bit to help us understand where these guys were coming from.

At that time in history, Israel was occupied by Rome. It's difficult for most of us to identify with that experience, since no foreign country has occupied the United States in our lifetimes. We've never had enemy soldiers walking up and down the street, telling us what we can and can't do. The Israelites hated being occupied by Rome and dreamed of the day they could be free from their presence.

And there was hope.

The Old Testament includes Messianic prophecies—more than three hundred of them—that foretold a Messiah who would come for the people one day. These prophecies said He would make lame people walk, cause blind people to see, and set prisoners free.

Many people misinterpreted these prophecies to mean that the Messiah foretold in the Old Testament would be a political Messiah who would set them free from Roman occupation and restore Israel to its "glory days." They didn't realize the Messiah would have an even greater goal in mind—a spiritual revolution, not a political one.

Even Jesus' closest followers sometimes got things mixed up, thinking He would bring political salvation. That's why James and John asked Him if they could sit on His right and left when He came into His Kingdom—they were still stuck on His being a political figure.

It's pretty clear now, as we look back, that Jesus had greater plans for these men than they had for themselves.

They wanted to be temporarily set free from Rome, but Jesus wanted to set them free from hell for eternity.

They wanted to be set free from the kingdom of Caesar; Jesus wanted to set them free from the kingdom of Satan.

They wanted to be set free from fear of Roman soldiers; Jesus wanted to set them free from fear of death, hell, and the grave.

As we look back with the advantage of being able to see the big picture, we can shake our heads at these two guys and wonder how in the world they didn't understand that Jesus had greater plans all along. We may even want to pull them aside and scold them for not trusting Him.

God as a Promise Keeper

Before we pass any more judgment on these two guys, however, we should do some self-reflection and admit that many times we are guilty of the same thing. We claim we can't trust Jesus because He didn't do what He said He'd do, when in actuality what we thought He said was really what *we* said.

Jesus is worthy of our complete trust—not just in some things, but in everything. He may not do what we hope He'll do. But that's only because our hopes are so small compared to what He wants to do in our lives and in this world.

> If our situation ain't good, then it ain't over!

We see in the Bible that God is not only a promise maker but also a promise keeper. Here's one of the many promises recorded in Scripture: "We know that God causes everything to work together for the good of those who love God and are called according to his purpose for them" (Romans 8:28). This means that all of us who love God can rest assured that if our situation ain't good, then it ain't over!

Jesus always has greater plans for us than we have for ourselves.

Let's pick up where we left off in the story. This is what the men said to Jesus:

> Some women from our group of his followers were at his
> tomb early this morning, and they came back with an amazing
> report. They said his body was missing, and they had seen angels
> who told them Jesus is alive! Some of our men ran out to see,
> and sure enough, his body was gone, just as the women had said.
> LUKE 24:22-24

They didn't recognize Jesus or believe in the resurrection, not only because of the pace of their lives, but also because they were so focused on their disappointment that they missed the miracle.

But Jesus met them where they were and brought them to where they needed to be. "Jesus said to them, 'You foolish people! You find it so hard to believe all that the prophets wrote in the Scriptures'" (Luke 24:25).

It's important to note something in this passage. When I'm reading the Bible, I try to notice not just the words but also the punctuation. And I pay special attention whenever I see an exclamation mark, because the writer is making it obvious that this point needs to be emphasized.

Did you catch the exclamation mark after Jesus' words? "You foolish people!" Clearly He wasn't trying to drop them a word of encouragement here but rather had begun to passionately proclaim the truth to them. He continued, "'Wasn't it clearly predicted that the Messiah would have to suffer all these things before entering his glory?' Then Jesus took them through the writings of Moses and all the prophets, explaining from all the Scriptures the things concerning himself" (Luke 24:26-27).

In other words, Jesus brought people who had been walking away from Him back to His presence through His Word.

Reading the Bible isn't just a good idea or something we should do when we have time. Rather, it's the main way we stay connected to God and keep our eyes fixed on Him. It's nearly impossible to walk away from someone when we have our eyes focused on that person.

And there is no greater way to focus on Jesus than through reading the Bible.

As Jesus took these men through the Old Testament passages that pointed to the Messiah, He revealed to them that it wasn't that God had let them down but rather that their perception of God was off.

I know that every time I've been disappointed in God, it's been the result of my misperceptions, not because He didn't come through on one of His promises.

God is a promise maker and a promise keeper—always has been, always will be!

CHAPTER 25

TRUST STRUGGLE #3: SPIRITUAL BLINDNESS

Here in the United States, most of us don't know much about savoring meals together for two or three hours. Shoot, if a restaurant takes two or three hours to get my food for me, I'm tempted to start throwing things. We don't want to sit down and "enjoy" the meal; we want to fly into the drive-thru and eat in the car on the way to our next appointment.

But that's not the way things were in the culture Jesus lived in.

> By this time they were nearing Emmaus and the end of their journey. Jesus acted as if he were going on, but they begged him, "Stay the night with us, since it is getting late." So he went home with them.
>
> LUKE 24:28-29

These guys were essentially asking Jesus to stay for a meal, and this would have been an invitation to an intimate setting. In Jesus' day, meals were slow paced—a time for conversation with family and trusted friends.

As the story develops, something strange takes place: "As they sat down to eat, he took the bread and blessed it. Then he broke it and gave it to them. Suddenly, their eyes were opened, and they recognized him. And at that moment he disappeared!" (Luke 24:30-31).

Why did they finally recognize Jesus at this point?

I believe I know. When Jesus walked the men through the prophecies about Him in the Old Testament, He surely would have quoted the prophecy from Isaiah that says, "He was pierced for our rebellion" (Isaiah 53:5). Surely He talked about the prophecy in Zechariah that says, "They will look on me whom they have pierced" (Zechariah 12:10). Keep in mind that key word *pierced*.

By this point in the story, these two men had slowed down the pace of their lives. They were no longer walking as fast as they could down the road with their own agenda. And they weren't struggling with their disappointment anymore, now that they'd spent a few hours going through Scripture with Jesus and having Him explain what they needed to know about Him and their current situation.

Then Jesus reached out and took hold of the bread to break it.

Hold on!

Think about this for a second: here these two men were seated in front of Jesus, and then He reached out His hands, took the bread, and broke it. And that's when they recognized Him.

Question: What was it that they saw that they hadn't seen when they were walking on the road?

Answer: The nail marks in His hands!

When they slowed down long enough to see His hands and they had spent time in the Word so they could truly understand who He was, their eyes were opened and they knew that Jesus could be completely trusted.

They said to each other, "Didn't our hearts burn within us as he talked with us on the road and explained the Scriptures to us?" And within the hour they were on their way back to Jerusalem. There they found the eleven disciples and the others who had gathered with them, who said, "The Lord has really risen! He appeared to Peter."

Then the two from Emmaus told their story of how Jesus had appeared to them as they were walking along the road, and how they had recognized him as he was breaking the bread.

LUKE 24:32-35

Notice two things about this passage: first of all, it's impossible to have a genuine encounter with Jesus and remain passive or apathetic about it afterward. These men went from not believing they could trust Him to being willing to retrace a seven-mile walk to tell people that what they'd previously heard about Jesus was true.

The second thing we notice in verse 35 is that the guys tell the other disciples that it was in the breaking of the bread—when they saw Jesus' hands—that they recognized Him.

When we see Jesus clearly, we will follow Him closely.

When we see Jesus clearly, we will follow Him closely. But we will never do so until we slow down the pace in our lives and get to the place where we trust His promises more than our preferences.

What about you?

Do you need to slow down the pace of your life so you can recognize Him?

Do you need to stop for a second and consider that maybe God didn't give you what you asked for because He had something greater in mind?

Do you need to ask the Lord to remove any spiritual blinders that are hindering your ability to see Him clearly?

Most anxiety and stress in our lives can be traced back to a point where we decided we were going to take control rather than believe that God is in control. When we see the nail marks in His hands, as the travelers on the road to Emmaus did, we begin to understand that the One who gave His life for us can be completely trusted—not just with some things, but with everything.

CHAPTER 26

DOES GOD
REALLY LOVE ME?

Every one of us loves someone or something.

For example, I love driving by Krispy Kreme doughnuts, seeing the "Hot Now" sign lit up, and going in to get several hot, fresh doughnuts along with the coldest glass of milk I can find.

I love watching the sun setting over the ocean.

I love college football (and I'd love it even more if they would develop a true play-off system!).

I love my wife and my daughter.

I could go on and on, but you get the point. I'd be willing to bet that if I asked you to list five people or things you love, you'd have no problem listing them right now.

However, when we bring in the true definition of love, that list may change a bit.

Here's the thing: love is determined by what we're willing to seek out and what we're willing to sacrifice for. Period.

We may be willing to seek out certain things, but that alone doesn't mean we love them. Love always requires sacrifice.

Let's say I'm sitting in my living room, craving a dozen hot Krispy Kreme doughnuts—so much so that I'm willing to get in my car and drive several miles to get them. However, when I walk into the store, I find that there's been a worldwide doughnut shortage, thus causing the price of doughnuts to increase to $500 a box.

There my "love" for doughnuts ends. Because while I would be willing to seek them out, I'd refuse to sacrifice $500 of my hard-earned money just to eat a few.

It's the same with college football. In my opinion, there's nothing like a great college football game, and I try to take my family to several college football games every year. I love to hear the band, watch the fans, and see two teams really go at it. I'm willing to seek out the experience—to sit in traffic for hours, walk through crowds of people, and pay money to get tickets and park.

And I love it.

However, if the news came out that we'd now have to sit in traffic for a minimum of four hours and the tickets would be $1,000 apiece, I would have to draw the line. I say I love college football, but if the price became too high, I wouldn't sacrifice the time and money to continue to be a fan. Therefore, what I have is not love.

On the other hand, let's say my daughter, Charisse, went missing. I wouldn't be passive or hesitate for a moment about that. I would look for her everywhere I could think of, and I wouldn't rest. I would vigorously pursue any leads to find her. And I wouldn't care what it cost me to get her back—time, money, or even my life. I love her enough not only to seek her out but also to sacrifice for her.

Obstacles to Accepting God's Love

Love is determined by what we're willing to seek out and what we're willing to sacrifice for.

With that definition of love in mind, I want you to know without a shadow of a doubt that God loves you. Without question, without condition.

If you're feeling bogged down by stress, let me fill you in on a secret: one of the best ways to overcome anxiety is to understand and accept God's love for you. Many people have a hard time believing that's true.

We may believe that God loves other people, but we have trouble believing He could love *us*.

One reason some of us have a hard time believing God loves us is because of past sins. Maybe before you came to Christ, you did some things that you aren't proud of. You try not to think about them, and you definitely don't talk about them. But even so, those past sins come up, and they bring with them overwhelming feelings of frustration, condemnation, and hopelessness.

How could God love me after what I did? you wonder.

Or maybe you did something you regret after you came to Christ. You met Jesus and walked with Him for a while, but for some reason you strayed off course and made some decisions that you knew were wrong. You've since come back to Him, but you're having a really hard time accepting that He loves you.

He might have loved me at one time, you think, *but there's no way He could love me after I turned my back on Him.*

Another reason we wrestle with believing that God loves us is because of our performance.

You may not struggle with a shady past. You may have been born to Christian parents, in church, on the altar. As soon as you came into this world, the first words out of your mouth were the Lord's Prayer, and immediately after that, you were baptized, served communion, and ordained into the ministry.

Okay, maybe that's a little extreme, but you get what I'm saying. As you look back over your past, there has never been a time when you really strayed from God. However, you struggle to accept God's love for you.

We live in a world that puts so much pressure on us to perform. From the time we enter school, join extracurricular activities, and go into the work world, everything we do is judged on our performance. If we do well, we get rewarded; if we do poorly, we get penalized. As a result, many of us have hopped onto the performance treadmill. We spend our lives trying our best to keep up with other people's unrealistic expectations.

And believe it or not, there is a religious treadmill too.

We look around us at church and see so many people who are better than we are. No matter how much we read the Bible, there are other people who read it more. No matter how much we pray, there's always someone who prays longer and better and more successfully than we do. And so we fall into the lie that God must love other people for their stellar performance, but there's no way He loves us because we just keep falling short of what others say we should be doing.

> **God has never brought anyone to a situation that was greater than His love for them.**

Other times we doubt God's love because of our present circumstances. We feel overwhelmed because of the suffering we are going through—sickness, financial stress, the death of someone close to us, the end of a relationship—and we wonder how in the world someone could say God loves us when all this pain is so prominent in our lives.

Love in the Presence of Lions

To really dig into this concept, let's take another look at the life of Daniel. No doubt there were times when he scratched his head and wondered if he'd done something wrong. It seems he kept hopping from one awful circumstance to another. And yet as we read his story, we see that he never vocally doubted the love of God.

If you are from a churched culture, then I'm sure you've heard the story of Daniel in the lions' den. If you haven't, you can find the entire story in Daniel 6. Long story short, Daniel had been serving the Babylonian government for quite a while and had earned so much power and influence that he was about to receive a major promotion.

But the local guys who worked with him were jealous, so those bone-heads made up a bogus law that if anyone prayed to a god other than the king over the next thirty days, they'd be thrown into a den of lions.

But Daniel didn't freak out, melt down, or give up. The Bible says,

"When Daniel learned that the law had been signed, he went home and knelt down as usual in his upstairs room, with its windows open toward Jerusalem. He prayed three times a day, just as he had always done, giving thanks to his God" (Daniel 6:10).

Daniel didn't doubt God's love, even in the most difficult of times. And the Lord saw him through his seeming crisis of spending an entire night with a group of hungry lions. Here's what Daniel said to the king the next morning: "My God sent his angel to shut the lions' mouths so that they would not hurt me, for I have been found innocent in his sight" (Daniel 6:22).

When we face our own lions, we can know that God's love for us is greater than whatever we're going through. And as we walk through the tough times, our view of Him will increase and our faith in Him will grow stronger.

God has never brought anyone to a situation that was greater than His love for them.

Not anyone in the Bible.

Not you—whatever situation you're facing right now.

Daniel probably didn't feel very loved by God as he was hanging out with the lions, but I imagine as the night went on, he grew to understand that God's love for him was greater than what threatened to devour him.

And the same is true for you. God is bigger than your lions.

CHAPTER 27

THE ONE JESUS LOVED

Something has always puzzled me about John, the writer of the fourth Gospel. In his book, John gives himself a nickname. Now if you give someone else a nickname, that's acceptable, but if you give *yourself* a nickname . . . well, that's just a little weird.

And when you consider John's nickname for himself, it hits the very top of the weird-o-meter.

On five separate occasions in his book, he refers to himself as "the disciple Jesus loved" or "the one whom Jesus loved."

How weird is that?

What if you ran into someone you knew at Walmart this afternoon, and when you called them by name, their reply was, "I would prefer that you use my nickname from now on. It's one I gave myself. You can just call me the one Jesus loves."

Let's be honest—you'd probably walk away thinking that person was about three pickles short of a full jar!

When I first read John's nickname, I wondered if he was being arrogant. It was like he was saying, "Jesus loves everyone, but I'm His favorite!"

Before we get into John's story, however, we need to back up and talk briefly about the Gospels. As I mentioned earlier, these four accounts about the life of Jesus can be found at the beginning of the New Testament. They go by the names of their authors: Matthew, Mark, Luke, and John.

Now stay with me as I give you a little background here, because it's important to appreciate this next part to understand where we're going. The books of Matthew, Mark, and Luke were written between AD 50 and AD 65. The Gospel of John, however, was written around AD 90—a couple of decades after the first three Gospels.

Think about this: by the time John wrote his book, he would have known about (and most likely read) what Matthew, Mark, and Luke had written about him. He would have known the things that had been said about him, the stories that had been told about him, and as we are going to see in the chapters that follow, he probably would have been aware that he came off as not very lovable.

Here's the key to unlocking this mystery: John wasn't bragging about himself. Instead, he was boasting about Jesus.

> **God's love is not based on *our* goodness; it's based on *His* goodness.**

"The one whom Jesus loves" is a description referring not to John's goodness, but to God's goodness.

The same is true for us: God's love is not based on *our* goodness; it's based on *His* goodness.

The Leftovers

To understand John, we need to know a little bit about the culture he was raised in. The Jewish school system two thousand years ago and our school system today look pretty much nothing alike. First of all, little girls weren't allowed to go to school—it was a boys-only club. Second, there were no coloring books and crayons, Dora movies, or craft times. The school systems back then were run by religious leaders—rabbis— and the goal of the school was to see who had what it took to be a future religious leader in the nation of Israel.

So from the age of five up to about eleven or twelve, little boys would memorize the first five books of the Bible. Some might argue that an assignment like that is simply impossible. A bunch of snot-nosed kids repeating back thousands of words verbatim? However, we must keep in mind that those kids didn't have to deal with the distractions kids today deal with. They had no iPads, Facebook accounts, or Twitter followers. Besides, the human mind has the ability to memorize a lot of information—it just depends on what we put into it. I'm sure we all have favorite movies that we've memorized key lines from because we've seen them so many times. (I'm not sure what this says about me, but I have numerous friends who can quote just about the entire movie of *Dumb and Dumber*.)

After this first level of schooling was complete, the religious leaders would select a group of students from the class who they believed had what it took to go to the next level in their studies. The rest were encouraged to go home and learn the trade of their fathers. For example, if a boy's father made shoes, then the son would learn how to make shoes as well so he could carry on the family business and take care of his family. If the father was a carpenter, then the son would learn the skills necessary to be a carpenter. You get the picture.

Then, after the top tier of students finished their second level of schooling (in which they would memorize the rest of the Old Testament), the leaders would once again select a group to continue on for training, while the ones who didn't have what it took would return home and learn the family trade.

I can't tell you how many times I've had people tell me they doubted God's love for them because they didn't believe there was anything special about them.

"Perry, I can't sing, I can't teach," they've told me. "I don't even know all the books of the Bible or the twelve apostles. Why in the world would Jesus love me?"

But remember, love is based on what we're willing to seek out and what we're willing to sacrifice for.

Now let's take a look at what happened when Jesus called His first disciples. "One day as Jesus was walking along the shore of the Sea of

Galilee, he saw two brothers—Simon, also called Peter, and Andrew—throwing a net into the water, for they fished for a living. Jesus called out to them, 'Come, follow me, and I will show you how to fish for people!' And they left their nets at once and followed him" (Matthew 4:18-20).

The first time I read this, I remember thinking, *Thank you, Captain Obvious, for letting us know they fished for a living. Duh!* However, after more study, I began to understand that Matthew was pointing this out to let his audience know that at some point in their schooling, Peter and Andrew had been rejected. They'd been told they weren't good enough and were sent home to keep up the family business. They weren't the cream of the religious crop.

A Messy Job

At this point I need to make two statements about fishing. Many people will disagree with the first; no one will disagree with the second.

First, there's nothing exciting about fishing.

Stop arguing with me on this one! I'm right!

But Perry, you've never hooked a big one! you may be screaming in your mind.

And you would be right, because in order to hook "a big one," I would have to get out of a perfectly comfortable bed, put on really weird-looking clothes, walk through the woods to places where lots of spiders and snakes live, and then "be patient" as I waited on a big one to bite!

No thanks.

One time a guy tried to argue with me about this, and I finally asked him, "Why do you like fishing so much?"

"I get in my boat and get out on the lake around five o'clock in the morning," he told me. "The water is so smooth and so peaceful. No one is bothering me, and I can just sit there and relax."

I quickly pointed out that in his description he had said nothing about fishing and that it actually sounded like he just enjoyed getting away from his wife and kids!

The other truth about fishing is one we will all agree with: fishing is messy. A good fisherman is never clean.

And the smell . . . dang! There's a reason people never have fish-scented air fresheners in their cars!

But this is good news for those of us who think God could never love us because of how messy our lives have been. After all, the first people Jesus called were a couple of messy fishermen.

"I've been too bad of a sinner to follow Jesus," I've heard people say. However, as a friend of mine once said, being a sinner doesn't disqualify us from following Jesus; it's actually a prerequisite. The only people in the Bible who didn't think they were sinners and didn't believe they needed Jesus were the hypocritical Pharisees!

As these ordinary fishermen were doing their jobs, things started to get interesting. "A little farther up the shore he saw two other brothers, James and John, sitting in a boat with their father, Zebedee, repairing their nets. And he called them to come, too. They immediately followed him, leaving the boat and their father behind" (Matthew 4:21-22).

> **Being a sinner doesn't disqualify us from following Jesus; it's actually a prerequisite.**

This is where we meet John. He wasn't doing anything religious, godly, or exciting when he made his entrance onto the pages of Scripture. He was a guy who had been pushed away by religious society and told he wasn't good enough to go to the next level. And this was the guy Jesus came to and said, "Follow Me!"

How in the world does someone go from not knowing anything about Jesus to eventually writing a book about Him?

Simple: you follow Him every day, one step at a time and to the best of your ability.

It was in the middle of John's messiness that Jesus said to him, "Hey, man, I want you on My team!"

Jesus isn't looking for perfect people—after all, there aren't any. Jesus isn't looking for pretty people—in fact, the prettier they try to be on the outside, the more broken they tend to be on the inside. Jesus is simply looking for willing people.

John wasn't perfect.

John had issues.

And still Jesus looked at him and said, "I want you to follow Me."

John knew that God loved him, not because of his amazing religious performance but because of Jesus' relentless pursuit of him.

CHAPTER 28

JOHN'S ISSUE #1: SELF-RIGHTEOUSNESS

Before we can talk about John's issues, we need to establish something. Would you call yourself a "dog person"? You love dogs, and you have one or maybe even several. But then there's the next level of dog lovers, the ones I call "dog in the house" people.

Now hold on—I'm not making fun of "dog in the house" people. In fact, I really want a dog in the house—I always have. Lucretia, on the other hand, doesn't want a dog in the house at all. So we've decided to compromise: we don't have a dog in the house.

When I was ten, my family had an awesome dog that was half German shepherd and half Norwegian elkhound. I named him Vader, after Darth Vader in *Star Wars*. (I've always believed that was the best name for a dog ever.)

My dad was a "no dog in the house, at all, under any circumstances" type of guy.

There really wasn't any compromise about this subject at that point in my life either.

On several occasions I tried to get my dad to allow Vader to come into the house, but my dad always said no—often followed by a few expletives to make sure I fully understood the passion he was trying to convey.

One summer my mother and father were both at work, and we had a yard guy come by to cut our grass. Vader was still a puppy at the time and was bounding all over the yard, going up to the guy and his lawn mower and getting dangerously close to him while he was cutting the grass.

So the guy cut the engine and called me over. "You're going to need to take this dog in the house while I cut your grass," he said. "If you don't, this lawn mower is going to suck him in, cut him into a thousand pieces, and then spread him all over your yard!"

I was horrified!

A quick tip here: don't tell a ten-year-old boy who is extremely visual about the new doggie fertilizer that is about to be created if the dog isn't taken care of.

Needless to say, I took Vader in the house.

Big mistake!

Vader had not been in the house five minutes when he walked into the living room and proceeded to take the largest poop I've ever seen come out of a dog—right in the middle of our living room floor. (Keep in mind this was the late 1970s, and our living room had this amazing orange shag carpet.)

> Religion says, "Clean up your mess!" Jesus says, "I cleaned up your mess!"

My first thought was, *My dad is going to kill me!* I knew I was in major trouble and I was going to get punished. I had a hunch that Vader might even wind up missing.

Then my second thought was, *Wait, I can totally clean this up!* I quickly developed a plan that would take care of the problem once and for all.

Bigger mistake!

I got a bunch of paper towels, and without getting too graphic here, let's just say that the more I tried to clean, the bigger the mess became. Now instead of sitting on top of the carpet, the poop was actually smashed into the carpet.

But I wasn't done yet.

I had a brilliant idea. If you're going to clean up a mess, you need cleaning materials, right?

So I ran to the kitchen, looked under the sink where we kept all our cleaning supplies, and grabbed a bottle of Fantastic and a bottle of 409. These were household cleaners, so I reasoned that if I sprayed enough of this stuff on the mess, it would be cleaned up and Dad would never know about the present Vader had left on the living room floor.

I sprayed massive amounts of the cleaning supplies on the mess and began to scrub and scrub and scrub.

A quick note of information that would have been helpful to me at the time: both of those cleaners contained bleach. So as I cleaned up Vader's poop, I also literally scrubbed the orange right out of the carpet. So now instead of having dog mess in our living room, there was a big white spot in the middle of our orange carpet.

Maybe my dad won't notice, I thought.

He noticed.

I've thought about that incident many times since then and concluded that we often do the same thing as Christians. We know we've made a mess at some point in our past. We don't argue about whether it's a mess—the mess is very clear to everyone. So we try to clean it up by being good and doing the right things.

This is called religion.

Religion says, "Clean up your mess!"

Jesus says, "I cleaned up your mess!"

That's a huge difference. When we feel like we have to clean up our mess, the stress and anxiety that go along with that responsibility can be overwhelming.

I believe that John struggled with this feeling himself.

We don't know much about what John's life was like before he met Christ. We don't know his habits or the things he'd done that he wasn't particularly proud of. But after he met Jesus, he did something all of us have done to try to get God's attention and impress Him.

In Luke 9:49, John said to Jesus, "Master, we saw someone using your name to cast out demons, but we told him to stop because he isn't in our group."

Notice that John went to Jesus and began to boast about what he'd done. It was like he was saying, "Hey, Jesus, I just did something awesome, and You need to know about it. You need to give me a gold star, tell me I'm special, and let everyone else know how awesome I am."

He wanted attention and affirmation from Jesus for his performance.

And we do the same thing.

Quick question: What in the world could any of us do to impress Jesus?

Answer: Nothing at all!

However, we still feel compelled to let God and other people know about all the important things we're doing. And when other people talk about their walks with God, we feel pressure to top it. If they say, "I read my Bible for ten minutes this morning," we feel the need to reply, "Well, I read mine for twenty-five!"

Comparing ourselves to others always makes us feel overwhelmed spiritually.

John was boasting about his accomplishment—most likely because he still couldn't believe that Jesus would call him out of his messy lifestyle. So he sought to try to justify himself.

And how did Jesus respond? "Jesus said, 'Don't stop him! Anyone who is not against you is for you'" (Luke 9:50).

Self-righteousness always gets a rebuke from Jesus. Jesus always redirects our focus to His work, not our own.

Take it from someone who has been there: self-righteousness only succeeds in smearing the mess around until you're even worse off than before.

And guess what? We don't have to clean up what Jesus paid for!

It's not our work that makes the difference in our relationship with Him; it's *His* work.

CHAPTER 29

JOHN'S ISSUE #2: SELFISHNESS

Okay, time for an honest question: Has there been at least one time in your life when you struggled with road rage? Someone cuts you off in traffic or they pull out in front of you and then drive as slowly as possible, and suddenly you feel the veins in your neck bulging. We have to admit that if we knew we'd get away with it, we might even do some serious damage to the car of the person who makes us angry!

When we get mad, we tend to act in ways that are not exactly righteous. That's when our selfish side rears its head.

With that visual of road rage in mind, let's read about another event that happened in the life of "the one whom Jesus loved."

As the time drew near for him to ascend to heaven, Jesus resolutely set out for Jerusalem. He sent messengers ahead to a Samaritan village to prepare for his arrival. But the people of the village did not welcome Jesus because he was on his way to Jerusalem. When James and John saw this, they said to Jesus, "Lord, should we call down fire from heaven to burn them up?"

LUKE 9:51-54

Uh, does anyone see a problem here?

The brothers James and John go to a village that doesn't want Jesus or His followers there. So John huddles everyone together and says, "Okay, I have an incredible plan that I think will work. Why don't we kill everyone in the village by calling down fire on it?"

This is what John, the disciple Jesus loved, was saying: "Let's burn them up!"

Can we admit that John had some serious issues at this point? What he wanted to do was both uncalled-for and ungodly.

And Jesus called him out on it: "Jesus turned and rebuked them" (Luke 9:55).

Wow, the one Jesus loved was definitely giving Him plenty of reasons to not love him.

The night before Jesus' crucifixion, there's another example of John's humanness. Even after following Jesus for several years, he still didn't get it.

> [Jesus] took some bread and gave thanks to God for it. Then he broke it in pieces and gave it to the disciples, saying, "This is my body, which is given for you. Do this to remember me."
>
> After supper he took another cup of wine and said, "This cup is the new covenant between God and his people—an agreement confirmed with my blood, which is poured out as a sacrifice for you.
>
> "But here at this table, sitting among us as a friend, is the man who will betray me. For it has been determined that the Son of Man must die. But what sorrow awaits the one who betrays him." The disciples began to ask each other which of them would ever do such a thing.
>
> LUKE 22:19-23

This was an incredibly intimate moment between Jesus and those who were closest to Him, and these are some of the most direct and passionate words He ever shared.

Then, just after Jesus told them that He was going to die, we see one of the most unbelievable verses in the Bible: "They began to argue among themselves about who would be the greatest among them" (Luke 22:24).

Really?

Right after they'd heard about all that Jesus was going to do, they started arguing about who was the greatest?

And John was right in the middle of that argument; after all, we read in the other Gospel accounts of this story that he was sitting right next to Jesus.

We also see indications of John's selfish perspective in this account:

> James and John, the sons of Zebedee, came over and spoke to him. "Teacher," they said, "we want you to do us a favor."
>
> "What is your request?" he asked.
>
> They replied, "When you sit on your glorious throne, we want to sit in places of honor next to you, one on your right and the other on your left."
>
> But Jesus said to them, "You don't know what you are asking! Are you able to drink from the bitter cup of suffering I am about to drink? Are you able to be baptized with the baptism of suffering I must be baptized with?"
>
> "Oh yes," they replied, "we are able!"
>
> Then Jesus told them, "You will indeed drink from my bitter cup and be baptized with my baptism of suffering. But I have no right to say who will sit on my right or my left. God has prepared those places for the ones he has chosen."
>
> MARK 10:35-40

These two passages point to something in John that we all have in ourselves: selfishness.

I know this firsthand.

For example, I am *not* a food sharer.

No, you cannot have a few of my fries.

No, you cannot have a bite of my sandwich.

It's mine—it belongs to me!

The exception to this policy, of course, is Lucretia.

From time to time, Lucretia and I will split a dessert in a restaurant. However, even with her, I draw an imaginary line through the middle of the dessert, and if she comes past that line, I get angry.

There's no denying it. I'm selfish.

If you've ever flown on an airplane, it's immediately obvious how selfish people are. What happens every time the little bell dings after the airplane lands and taxis into place? Everyone stands up at the same time and crowds into the aisle, trying to be the first off the plane. It's one of the most frustrating parts about traveling.

Several months ago I decided I was going to turn over a new leaf— that I was going to be unselfish in this area of my life. Rather than jumping up and trying to be first, I was going to stay seated and allow everyone else to go in front of me.

My resolution was tested when Lucretia and I went out of town for a long weekend. When our plane landed in Atlanta and the bell indicated that we could stand up, I remained seated. A large man in the seat next to me stood up immediately, and when I turned my head to the right, his rear end was right in my face. It was, hands down, one of the most uncomfortable situations I've ever been in.

I turned to complain to Lucretia, and she instructed me to calm down.

And that's when *it* happened.

The lady in front of the large man asked if she could get by him to get her bag, and this dude literally sat down on my shoulder!

I told Lucretia that I was about to break someone off, and she proceeded to tell me that I was going to behave.

I kept telling myself, *This is what happens when you're unselfish—you stare at someone's rear end and get sat on all day long!* At least that's how I felt, because I was still focused on me.

John was focused on himself, and that caused issues for him too.

Did you know that almost every problem in marriage is caused by the selfishness of one or both people?

Did you know that nearly every financial problem begins with selfishness?

Did you know that practically every strained relationship at work or in a family can be traced back to selfishness?

Maybe this is an issue you wrestle with. As you look back over your life, you realize that some of the decisions you made were completely selfish, and because of those decisions, you think there's no way God could ever love you.

> **If Jesus could love John through his selfishness, then He can love us through ours.**

The divorce . . .

The wayward child . . .

The lost money . . .

The sexual encounters outside of marriage . . .

You did something you regret because you wanted something in the moment.

But remember, John demonstrated selfishness too, yet he was the disciple Jesus loved. If Jesus could love John through his selfishness, then He can love us through ours.

We will always wrestle with selfish desires. The battle is not whether we will have selfish tendencies but rather what we will do with those desires—whether we will allow what we desire in the moment to trump what we ultimately want.

Being unselfish means disciplining ourselves to say yes to the Lord even when we want to tell Him no.

CHAPTER 30

A FRIEND OF GOD

Scripture says that when Jesus was arrested, all the disciples ran away—but John didn't totally desert his Lord. The Bible records that John went to the place where Jesus had to stand before the high priest. He saw Jesus condemned to die, he saw Him take a beating, and he was the only disciple present at the Crucifixion.

And although that might have put him one step ahead of the other disciples, the truth is that even though John chose to be near Jesus, he still didn't speak up and identify with Him. John chose to be cautious when he could have been courageous. He chose to be silent when he could have taken a stand.

And truthfully, that's what some of us have done as well. We've gotten close to Jesus but never really identified with Him.

Maybe unethical practices were happening at work and you knew you should speak out against them, but rather than taking a stand, you stayed silent because you didn't want to be labeled. And as a result, you believe there's no way Jesus could love you.

Or maybe you were with someone in an intimate moment when the mood was "right" and things began to progress too far physically. You knew you shouldn't do it, but if you said anything, you were afraid the relationship would suffer. So you allowed something to happen that you knew shouldn't have happened, and you think God will never love you now.

At some point we've all felt like we've let God down. And the fear that we've lost His love and approval brings about unreal amounts of stress and anxiety. We don't know what to do with all the guilt we feel.

Falling Back on Our Old Ways

In John 20, we read that Jesus rose from the dead and appeared to the disciples. He told them He was sending them into the world to declare the message that He is alive and that there is hope.

However, the disciples weren't completely convinced that He was over the whole "We ran away from you, denied you, and never really identified with you" thing.

> Jesus appeared again to his disciples, by the Sea of Galilee. It happened this way: Simon Peter, Thomas (also known as Didymus), Nathanael from Cana in Galilee, the sons of Zebedee, and two other disciples were together. "I'm going out to fish," Simon Peter told them, and they said, "We'll go with you." So they went out and got into the boat, but that night they caught nothing.
>
> JOHN 21:1-3, NIV

Quick question: What had John been doing before he met Jesus? Answer: Fishing! Because he was a fisherman.

But then everything changed. He met Jesus, walked with Him for three years, and saw miracles he'd never imagined. And then, all of a sudden, he was back where he'd been before he met Jesus, doing the same things he'd been doing before he met Jesus.

And maybe that's where you are right now too.

Maybe you used to read your Bible a lot and go to church. Maybe you stopped doing things you knew weren't good for you and began living a different life.

But something happened. You made one bad decision that led to a series of bad decisions, and now you're at a place you thought you'd never return to, doing the same things you did before you met Christ.

Some people would tell you that you never actually met Jesus. Others might argue that there's no way you can ever be close to Him again. And you feel like there's no way He could ever love you again because, well, you blew it! You believe that Jesus may have loved you "back when," but there's no way He loves you right now.

Maybe things just aren't like they used to be.

There was a time when you saw the Lord so clearly and you heard His voice almost daily, but you've gotten to the point where you just aren't sure He's even speaking anymore.

> **Like the disciples who went fishing, without Jesus, we will catch nothing.**

If this is you, you're not alone. In the text we see that these guys who had spent three years with Jesus and knew His voice didn't even recognize Him when He appeared on the shore and began to speak to them.

Something interesting happened when the disciples went back to fishing: "They went out and got into the boat, but that night they caught nothing" (John 21:3, NIV).

We walk away from Jesus because we fall for the lie that He is holding out on us and that we can experience more joy by seeking our own satisfaction instead of His presence. But the Bible says that when the disciples went back to what they used to do, they caught nothing.

Without Jesus, we will catch nothing. The world can only provide us with false hope and temporary satisfaction. True joy comes through an active, ongoing walk with Christ. And wherever you are, however long you've been gone, it's not too late for you!

Still His Friends

Before we can understand the significance of what happened when the disciples encountered Jesus on the shore, we need to look back at Jesus' words to them the night before He was crucified. This is what He said after He shared Communion with His guys.

> Greater love has no one than this: to lay down one's life for one's *friends*. You are my *friends* if you do what I command. I no longer call you servants, because a servant does not know his master's business. Instead, I have called you *friends*, for everything that I learned from my Father I have made known to you.
>
> JOHN 15:13-15, NIV, EMPHASIS ADDED

Jesus called them His friends! And He didn't just say it once—He said it three separate times. He used the word *friends* on purpose. He knew they were going to abandon and deny Him. He knew they were going to go back to what they'd done before they met Him. And He still called them His friends.

Now let's return to the last chapter of John.

> Early in the morning, Jesus stood on the shore, but the disciples did not realize that it was Jesus.
>
> He called out to them, *"Friends*, haven't you any fish?"
>
> JOHN 21:4-5, NIV, EMPHASIS ADDED

Did you catch that emphasized word? He called them friends again!

Some have said that the miracle in this chapter is about the catching of the fish. However, I think it's about John recognizing that Jesus sought out the disciples and sacrificed His life for them.

And even though they'd changed their minds about Jesus in a moment of uncertainty and fear, He hadn't changed His mind about them.

The name He called them when they went back to fishing was the same name He'd called them before they ran away. *Friends!*

It's one thing to call someone a friend when you're sitting around a table with bread and wine and sharing an intimate moment. But these guys had walked away from Jesus, denied Him, even cursed Him. And yet He sought them out—not to get back at them, but rather to bring them back into a relationship with Him.

If you're currently not as close to Jesus as you once were, then I pray you will understand that He's trying to bring you, too, back into a relationship with Him. He sacrificed His life for you, and He has sought you out.

These verses offer a striking picture of God's love:

> I am convinced that nothing can ever separate us from God's love. Neither death nor life, neither angels nor demons, neither our fears for today nor our worries about tomorrow—not even the powers of hell can separate us from God's love. No power in the sky above or in the earth below—indeed, nothing in all creation will ever be able to separate us from the love of God that is revealed in Christ Jesus our Lord.
>
> ROMANS 8:38-39

John was "the disciple Jesus loved," which says a lot more about Jesus than it does about John.

Because John was the former messy fisherman.

The guy who kept bragging about himself.

The guy who thought it was a good idea to wipe out an entire village.

The guy who was so obsessed with himself that he couldn't hear Jesus say He was about to give His life for him.

The guy who walked back to what he used to do and who he once was before he met Christ.

And yet Jesus loved John.

And that's true for you, too!

Don't allow the religious world to tell you that God's love is something you can earn or achieve. The pressure associated with that lie is crippling. God's love is something we receive, and it can never be taken from us.

This reality came crashing down on me on my last trip to Israel.

One of the sites you can visit while you're there is a place called Peter's Primacy. It's the place where people believe this story from John 21 took place.

It was cool the day we were there, with a slight wind blowing off the Sea of Galilee. I had some time to sit beside the little church that has been built there and stare out at the water.

Before I came to Christ, I did some things I'm not proud of. In fact, there are times when the condemnation I feel for what I've done has nearly crippled me emotionally.

As I sat in the place where Jesus pursued those who had walked away from Him, it hit me: Jesus knew every stupid, foolish, sinful decision I would ever make, and yet He still chose to create me, love me, pursue me, and rescue me.

In that same place where Jesus had pursued His disciples, I recognized that all my life He had been pursuing me, too—not to get back at me, but to bring me back to a place where I could walk with Him again.

If you're far away from Him right now, I invite you to join me on the shoreline and return to the One who has been pursuing you all along.

Doing this simply requires a willingness to stop doing what He's telling you to stop doing and a willingness to start doing what He says you need to start doing. When you follow Him, you will be able to get out of the pit that has held you for far too long and step into the amazing plans He has in mind for you.

CHAPTER 31

DON'T
GIVE UP

Last year I was in the Atlanta airport trying to catch a connecting flight to get home when I saw one of the craziest things I've ever witnessed in my life. Before I tell you what happened, though, let me describe the scene so you can get the full context.

The terminals in the Atlanta airport are all spread out, so if your plane lands in one terminal and you need to get to another one, you can do so either by taking a long walk or by riding a subway-like train.

On that particular day, I was in a hurry, so I headed for the train. Now something you should know about these trains is that there's a warning when the doors are about to close. A recorded voice comes over a loudspeaker and says something along the lines of "The train doors are about to close; please step away."

I boarded the train and waited for about a minute as people exited and entered, and then, sure enough, the recorded voice came over the loudspeaker and the doors began to close.

That's when it happened.

As the doors were closing, a rather large man leaped onto the train. Then he turned around and grabbed the hand of a woman who was somewhere in her seventies, trying to pull her onto the train. But it was too late—the doors closed on her, completely trapping her so she couldn't move.

The guy who had made the grand entrance pulled her arm, screaming, "Come on, Mom!" Then I saw a younger woman outside the train, pushing the little old lady from the other side.

About that time, an announcement came over the loudspeaker telling everyone to please step away from the doors.

I freaked out!

This poor woman couldn't step away from the doors because she was trapped in them. I just knew that any minute this train was going to take off and the woman with the not-so-bright children was going to be flapping all over the place as the train sped from one terminal to the next.

Finally, after what seemed like an eternity, the doors of the train opened again and the woman was set free. But the look on her face told quite a story about the overwhelming circumstances she'd just been through.

Later that night, when I was lying in bed, I thought about times in my own life when I'd felt a lot like that old lady.

Trapped.

Hopeless.

Scared to death about what was about to happen.

With people pushing me from one side and pulling me from the other.

With people yelling at me.

And with no promise of a way out.

I'm sure you've been there too. In fact, you may be there right now.

In times like these, one of the biggest temptations we face is to give up—to throw in the towel and call it quits.

When we're stuck there, the last thing we want to hear is how much God loves us, how powerful He is, and how He can save us from situations that stress us out. We think, *If that's true, then where in the heck is He right now?*

But what I've learned through personal experience as well as through my reading of Scripture is that we should never give up on the God who has never given up on us.

I imagine you're pushing back at this point, because it may seem that

God has given up, that He doesn't care, and that nothing in your life is ever going to get better. If anyone ever had a reason to feel that way, it had to be the Old Testament figure Job.

The book of Job is about a man who was, without a doubt, dominated by overwhelming circumstances. We will dive into some specifics about his story later, but first I want to take a look at the end of the book. The book of Job is fairly long, and it's easy to get bogged down and overlook some of the key truths tucked into the last couple of chapters. When I came across this verse recently, it hit me like a brick in the face: "The LORD blessed Job in the second half of his life even more than in the beginning" (Job 42:12).

> "The LORD blessed Job in the second half of his life even more than in the beginning." —Job 42:12

How in the world had I read this book so many times and never seen that verse? Had it always been there, or did someone sneak into my house in the middle of the night and add it to my Bible?

In sermons we usually hear about Job's overwhelming circumstances, but we don't pay as much attention to how his life actually ended. But sure enough, God blessed Job's life in the second half even more than He'd blessed it in the first.

I want that for my life. If God is handing out blessings, I want all He cares to pour out on me.

And I want that for you as well.

Maybe you want that too, but you can't believe it's possible for God to bless you right now. Your life was going along great, and then that one thing happened and everything took a turn for the worse. You feel like the woman trapped in the door, with no relief in sight. As a result, you feel frustrated with your marriage, your job, your kids, your parents . . . and maybe even God.

When we get frustrated, the easiest thing to do is give up. But the Bible has some words of encouragement for us when we find ourselves in this situation. One of the promises I find myself coming back to over and over again is from Galatians 6:9: "Let's not get tired of doing what is good. At just the right time we will reap a harvest of blessing if we don't give up."

Before we move on, let me acknowledge that you may not want to hear this right now. You may be saying, "Well, if God hasn't given up on me, why am I going through these circumstances? Why is my life this way? How in the world can you tell me that God hasn't given up on me?"

If that's how you're feeling, I've been there too. When I was battling depression and anxiety, the last thing I wanted was someone quoting Bible verses at me and telling me that God hadn't given up on me.

But stop for just a second and think about something. You just read a chapter about not giving up, right? If God really had given up on you, then how can you explain the fact that right now you have a book in your hands reminding you that God has great plans for you?

Coincidence?

No way!

God knew you before you were born. He has had a plan for you all along. And He just let you know He hasn't given up on you. So don't give up on Him!

CHAPTER 32

LIFE IS HARD

I wish this weren't the case, but it's true: life is hard. We live in a fallen world, and we experience the consequences of that reality every day.

I learned years ago that the sooner I accept this reality, the less surprised I'll be when tough times come, and the more likely I'll be to fight the temptation to throw in the towel.

None of us ever planned for a hard life; in fact, I'm quite sure nobody schedules their tragedies. "Lunch on Tuesday? No, I can't—I'm going to slam my car into an idiot who runs a red light around 11:15 that day, which means at that time I'll be in surgery that will hopefully save my life."

We assume life is going to be good. After all, advertisements promise us that if we buy their products or pay them a lot of money, our lives are guaranteed to turn out better than we ever imagined.

But it's not true. Life is hard—and it's hard even during those times when we think it's supposed to be awesome. I learned this firsthand when I took my wife and daughter to Disney World for the first time.

Disney has some pretty effective marketing, and it's easy to get completely sucked in. You see the TV commercials where Mickey Mouse is on Main Street, with no one around him. A family approaches him, and he hugs the children and walks hand in hand with them through the park. There's no wait for the rides. It's not hot. And all the children have smiles on their faces. What parents wouldn't want this for their children?

But if you are a parent and have ever been to Disney, you know that what is advertised and what is experienced are two completely different things.

> **Life is hard—and it's hard even during those times when we think it's supposed to be awesome.**

My family spent a week in the Magic Kingdom, and Lucretia and I like to refer to that trip as our week in the place of everlasting darkness where there is weeping and gnashing of teeth.

Mickey was not standing alone on Main Street—we had to stand in a line for an hour to see him.

The park was not empty—it was so crowded we could barely move.

At the end of the day, we were not a happy family bounding with energy and playfulness like the family we'd seen in the TV ad. Instead, we were the completely exhausted family carrying a passed-out four-year-old back to the room while calling the marriage counseling hotline.

If life is hard at Disney, there's no way we should expect our everyday lives to be a cakewalk.

What Job Had to Deal With

We first meet Job in Job 1:1-3.

> There once was a man named Job who lived in the land of Uz. He was blameless—a man of complete integrity. He feared God and stayed away from evil. He had seven sons and three daughters. He owned 7,000 sheep, 3,000 camels, 500 teams of oxen, and 500 female donkeys. He also had many servants. He was, in fact, the richest person in that entire area.

Here we see a guy who, based on external appearances, had everything going for him. The Bible says he was blameless, a man of complete integrity. And I would say he had a pretty decent relationship with his wife, given the fact that they had ten kids! In that society, you were considered blessed by God if you had lots of money, and clearly Job's situation wasn't too shabby, considering that the Bible says he was the richest person around.

Everything was going his way.

As we continue with the story, we see that Job was a pretty upstanding guy too.

> Job's sons would take turns preparing feasts in their homes, and they would also invite their three sisters to celebrate with them. When these celebrations ended—sometimes after several days—Job would purify his children. He would get up early in the morning and offer a burnt offering for each of them. For Job said to himself, "Perhaps my children have sinned and have cursed God in their hearts." This was Job's regular practice.
>
> JOB 1:4-5

Job loved his family. He loved God and had an ongoing relationship with Him. He was serious about doing what was right. He had it all together.

But then "it" happened—the one thing that completely changed the trajectory of his life.

> One day the members of the heavenly court came to present themselves before the LORD, and the Accuser, Satan, came with them. "Where have you come from?" the LORD asked Satan.
>
> Satan answered the LORD, "I have been patrolling the earth, watching everything that's going on."
>
> Then the LORD asked Satan, "Have you noticed my servant Job? He is the finest man in all the earth. He is blameless—a man of complete integrity. He fears God and stays away from evil."
>
> JOB 1:6-8

We've all seen moms with stickers on the back of their minivans that tell the world how perfect their children are. It's pretty much a universal fact that all parents love to brag on their kids. We see in these verses that God was bragging on His son Job. You have officially reached next-level status when God starts telling people how great you are!

That's when the trouble started.

Satan replied to the LORD, "Yes, but Job has good reason to fear God. You have always put a wall of protection around him and his home and his property. You have made him prosper in everything he does. Look how rich he is! But reach out and take away everything he has, and he will surely curse you to your face!"

JOB 1:9-11

God and Satan are not equals. They aren't locked in some cosmic struggle to see who is going to win. God is sovereign and supreme and owns the devil.

Satan flat-out rails on God and basically says, "Of course Job follows You—You've given him everything he wants and haven't allowed anything bad to happen to him. But if circumstances in his life changed—if overwhelming things hit him out of nowhere—he'd turn his back on You."

Here's how God responded:

"All right, you may test him," the LORD said to Satan. "Do whatever you want with everything he possesses, but don't harm him physically." So Satan left the LORD's presence.

JOB 1:12

Don't miss this! It's important to note that Satan had to get permission from God before he acted. God and Satan are not equals. They aren't locked in some cosmic struggle to see who is going to win. God is sovereign and supreme and owns the devil.

Which means that nothing has ever happened to us by accident—things are either caused by God or allowed by God. Make no mistake: nothing can take place in our lives without first passing through His hands.

As we continue with the story, we see that tragedy struck:

> One day when Job's sons and daughters were feasting at the oldest brother's house, a messenger arrived at Job's home with this news: "Your oxen were plowing, with the donkeys feeding beside them, when the Sabeans raided us. They stole all the animals and killed all the farmhands. I am the only one who escaped to tell you."
>
> While he was still speaking, another messenger arrived with this news: "The fire of God has fallen from heaven and burned up your sheep and all the shepherds. I am the only one who escaped to tell you."
>
> While he was still speaking, a third messenger arrived with this news: "Three bands of Chaldean raiders have stolen your camels and killed your servants. I am the only one who escaped to tell you."
>
> While he was still speaking, another messenger arrived with this news: "Your sons and daughters were feasting in their oldest brother's home. Suddenly, a powerful wind swept in from the wilderness and hit the house on all sides. The house collapsed, and all your children are dead. I am the only one who escaped to tell you."
>
> JOB 1:13-19

Talk about overwhelming circumstances! In the course of one day, Job went from being the richest guy in the neighborhood to being completely bankrupt. He went from having ten kids to being childless. I can't even imagine this type of pain. I tear up when my daughter skins her knee. We'd expect Job to wrestle with anger and frustration, believing that God had abandoned him.

But this is how Job responded:

Job stood up and tore his robe in grief. Then he shaved his head and fell to the ground to worship. He said,

"I came naked from my mother's womb,
    and I will be naked when I leave.
The LORD gave me what I had,
    and the LORD has taken it away.
Praise the name of the LORD!"

In all of this, Job did not sin by blaming God.
JOB 1:20-22

If this were the end of the story, it would be tragic enough. But somehow things manage to get even worse.

One day the members of the heavenly court came again to present themselves before the LORD, and the Accuser, Satan, came with them. "Where have you come from?" the LORD asked Satan.

Satan answered the LORD, "I have been patrolling the earth, watching everything that's going on."

Then the LORD asked Satan, "Have you noticed my servant Job? He is the finest man in all the earth. He is blameless—a man of complete integrity. He fears God and stays away from evil. And he has maintained his integrity, even though you urged me to harm him without cause."
JOB 2:1-3

If I were Job, I'd be yelling at God and at Satan at this point. "Would you two *please* quit talking about me? Every time you two talk, my life falls apart!"

But sure enough, the talking continued, and Job's life kept getting worse. God basically told Satan, "You lost!" and Satan replied, "Well, uh, let me take away his health, and then he'll turn his back on You."

Once again, God gave Satan permission to act, but what he was allowed to do was limited.

> "All right, do with him as you please," the LORD said to Satan. "But spare his life." So Satan left the LORD's presence, and he struck Job with terrible boils from head to foot.
>
> Job scraped his skin with a piece of broken pottery as he sat among the ashes.
>
> JOB 2:6-8

That stinks! I can't imagine the pain, hurt, and confusion Job must have been feeling at that point. Not long ago I sprained my ankle really bad, and I just about lost my mind. And that's nothing compared to what happened to Job. I mean, terrible boils from head to foot? Not pleasant. When our health starts to fall apart, it often causes us to question God and doubt His goodness.

And then, to make matters worse, the very person who was supposed to be supporting Job gave up hope herself.

> His wife said to him, "Are you still trying to maintain your integrity? Curse God and die."
>
> JOB 2:9

I don't know about you, but this is the point where I would have drawn the line. Job had lost all his money, his livelihood, his kids, his health . . . and now his wife came to him and basically said, "I wish you would die!"

When I read the book of Job for the first time, I remember thinking, *Man, Job would have been better off if God had left some of the animals alive and taken Job's wife out instead!*

Before we move on, though, I think we need to be fair to Mrs. Job. She was in the middle of completely overwhelming circumstances herself. She'd just lost all ten of her children and watched her husband go bankrupt, and now she was watching him die a slow death.

Then here's the icing on the cake: even his friends let him down.

At first these guys were silent and just sat with him, which is what we all need in times of trouble. However, it didn't take long for their self-righteousness to kick in, and instead of walking through this tough time with him, they began to lecture Job. Here's what one of his best friends actually said to him:

> Does God twist justice?
>   Does the Almighty twist what is right?
> Your children must have sinned against him,
>   so their punishment was well deserved.
>
> JOB 8:3-4

Wow. One of Job's "friends" really told him, "God killed your children, and they probably deserved it."

Maybe Job had been encouraged when he heard that his friends were going to stop by to cheer him up. But then, instead of encouraging him, they blasted him and his kids for some unknown sins!

Talk about a party.

At this point I would be saying to God, "Please kill me now!"

What You Have to Deal With

Life is hard, and most of the time we never even see "it" coming.

Maybe at this point you're expecting me to say something along the lines of "Your story isn't as bad as Job's, so shut up and get over it."

Stay calm—I'm not going there! I'm not going to tell you that the overwhelming circumstances you're experiencing aren't real. And I am not going to try to "out-pain" your pain.

Have you ever met someone like that?

Let's say you were doing some meal prep in the kitchen and accidentally cut your finger, causing you to have to go to the emergency room and get several stitches. The next day you run into a friend at the coffee shop and he says, "What's up with that bandage on your finger?"

You tell him about the accident and the ER experience, and then mention that it hurt pretty bad.

And then that friend says, "That's not pain! I'll tell you what pain is. Do you see my right leg? It's not my real leg. I was in the Amazon with a backpack of Bibles trying to reach an unreached people group when a storm came out of nowhere, causing a tree to fall on my leg and pin me to the ground. I couldn't move. But I was dedicated to reaching those people, so I took out my pocketknife and sawed off my leg. I didn't even whimper. I then took the knife and carved a leg out of the tree that had fallen on me. Then I went on and reached an entire tribe for Jesus. So don't tell me about your stupid finger!"

If you ever meet that person, I believe it's perfectly okay to punch him in the throat. But since that's not a permanent fix and we're bound to face some kind of pain at some point in our lives, we'll need to figure out biblical ways to deal with it.

CHAPTER 33

PAIN HAS A NAME

You don't need me to define pain for you—you already know what pain is. But it can be helpful to categorize the types of pain we deal with—all of which Job had to wrestle through himself.

Physical Pain

When Job's health was taken away, he suffered—really suffered. And maybe you have too.

I remember watching my mother, who had always been a picture of health, suffer with cancer. Perhaps worst of all was seeing her and my dad wrestle with their faith in God because of the pain she was going through.

Maybe you can relate. You thought you were perfectly healthy when you went to the doctor for a routine checkup, but then you received a call informing you that a mass had been found. And that single phone call altered the course of your entire life.

Physical pain can cause us to question God in a profound way. But God encourages us to come to Him with our wounds.

I am suffering and in pain.
Rescue me, O God, by your saving power.
PSALM 69:29

Emotional Pain

Can you imagine the emotional pain associated with losing all your children and believing you're a complete failure because your entire life's work has been wiped out in a single day?

I would say that most of us haven't had such a drastic experience in one day; however, we've all had to deal with emotional pain.

Maybe you lost a child.

Maybe you experienced sexual abuse in your past.

Maybe it was the miscarriage.

Maybe it was the lost job.

Maybe it was the divorce.

No matter what your specific situation, the pain you are going through is real.

I wish there was a way to avoid emotional pain. With physical pain, the damage is easily seen and can be attended to. However, with emotional pain, the scarring occurs on the inside—deep down, in a place we rarely let anyone see and seldom talk about. We even try to hide that pain from God, because we fear He can't handle our honesty.

But know this: God isn't afraid of your questions, your fears, or your doubts. He's bigger than all of them.

Financial Pain

Job lost every possession he had. This type of pain can be especially crippling to men, whose self-worth is often tied to their net worth. When something happens to impact their bottom line in a negative way, they feel helpless and defeated.

When the most recent recession hit our country, it was heartbreaking to see news stories about men who took their own lives—and sometimes the lives of their family members too—because they felt so hopeless. They were afraid they'd never escape the chains of their circumstances.

Nearly everyone reading this book has felt the reality of financial pain. It has the ability to rob us of joy and overshadow everything good we have in our lives. It's easy to neglect seeing all the good that God has done for us when we receive a bill in the mail we weren't expecting or when we aren't sure how we're going to provide for our families the way we want to.

Relational Pain

It doesn't take a therapist to see that Job and his wife were navigating through some tension in their marriage!

Every marriage goes through times when the struggles are intense. Have you ever wanted to give up on your spouse? Have you ever looked at that person, thought back on your wedding day, and asked yourself, *What was I thinking?* I've had many conversations with couples in which one spouse looks at the other and says, "I've been hurt so badly by what you've done that I can't take this anymore."

Job's wife wanted to give up on him, and though Scripture doesn't say this, I imagine Job didn't want to spend a lot of time around Mrs. Job. But as we will see, in the end they didn't give up on each other, and they were able to reconcile their relationship.

Maybe for you the painful relationship is not with a spouse but with a parent, a coworker, or someone you once thought of as a good friend.

The closer the relationship, the greater the potential for pain.

However, it's in these times that I have come to realize that God hasn't left me to deal with my pain alone. And His presence is greater than my pain.

Spiritual Pain

The false idea Job faced in his day still exists today—that God makes good things happen to good people and bad things happen to bad people. If you're good, if you dot your i's and cross your t's, then God will bless you. If you're bad, then God will make your tire go flat, your kids go crazy, or your marriage fall apart.

There are two problems with this idea: the first is Jesus, and the second is the Bible.

Well-intentioned people all too often try to reduce Christianity to little sayings and formulas that are absolutely ridiculous. Most of the "Christian" bumper stickers out there are pretty off base. The one that bothers me most, however, is the one that says, "The safest place to be is in the will of God."

Doesn't that sound so beautiful?

So poetic?

So inspirational?

But so *wrong*!

If the safest place to be is in the will of God, then what do we do with Jesus? No one on the planet has ever been more in the will of God than He was, and He wound up beaten, mocked, and crucified.

God's will is good, but it's anything but safe.

Job wasn't doing anything wrong. In fact, he was doing everything right. And in the first two chapters of the book, he had an outstanding attitude. However, he openly wrestled with God's goodness throughout the rest of the book, displaying an emotional roller coaster that included anger, confusion, and frustration. It's the same ride we've all been on when we go through tough times. Why? Because life is hard.

> **God's will is good, but it's anything but safe.**

One of the things that drives my wife crazy is when I stop to watch TV preachers when I'm flipping through the television channels. Please understand that I don't believe all TV preachers are bad; however, some drive me absolutely insane, because I believe that some of the things they teach are simply not true.

I've heard some of them say, "If you just believe in Jesus and have enough faith, then you won't ever get sick, have a bad day, or experience any sort of tragedy."

But once again, Jesus had more faith than anyone else who has ever walked this earth, and yet He wound up on a cross. Or take the martyrs, for example. Many of Jesus' disciples were killed because they refused to stop talking about Him. They had faith, and it cost them their lives.

Job's life is evidence of the truth of some of Jesus' final words to His disciples: "I have told you all this so that you may have peace in me. Here on earth you will have many trials and sorrows. But take heart, because I have overcome the world" (John 16:33). In other words, we will go through troubles, but that's not the end of the story.

> **In a world that is all bad, God is still all good.**

In a world that is all bad, God is still all good.

CHAPTER 34

GOD IS STILL GOD, AND GOD IS STILL GOOD

I'd dreamed of visiting Israel ever since I became a Christian in 1990. After doing some saving and investigating, I found a deal from a tour company that offered an all-inclusive preview trip. When I got my plane tickets, I was almost out of my mind with happiness to discover that my seat was in the business class section.

I'm not sure if you've ever been able to fly business class on an international flight, but I'm going to go ahead and tell you that it's an amazing experience. For starters, I had a seat that wasn't designed for an Oompa Loompa. Plus, the flight attendants gave me a big pillow, a blanket, little booties for my feet, and a hot towel.

Please understand that I'm just a redneck from South Carolina. In other words, I ain't used to all that!

As I sat there taking it all in, a flight attendant came by and handed me something. When I asked what it was, she replied, "It's a menu. We're going to serve you a meal as soon as we take off."

You've got to be kidding me! I thought. *This is awesome! I have a hot towel, a pillow, and booties, and they're going to feed me too?*

I selected the sirloin steak and then sat back. I was having the time of my life.

But the guy next to me—uh, not so much. For the sake of this story, we'll refer to him as Cletus. He looked like a Cletus, anyway. And it seemed that Cletus was having a very bad day, because from the moment he got on the plane, he was scowling.

Cletus ordered the steak too. And sure enough, after the plane took off, they brought us our steaks. My joy meter was just about maxed out.

Out of the corner of my eye, I saw Cletus cut into his steak, and let's just say it wasn't joy I saw on his face. He looked up and then looked at his steak again. Then he went completely crazy, throwing his silverware down and frantically pushing the flight attendant call button.

As the flight attendant headed toward Cletus, the first thing out of his mouth was, "Ma'am, I'm from Texas. . . ."

At this point I knew that whatever was about to go down would be far more interesting than the movie I was halfway paying attention to.

Cletus continued, "Where I come from, we order our steaks rare. This steak is not rare, and I demand that you bring me another steak."

I was a bit surprised at the apparent statewide mandate in Texas about how to prepare steak, and apparently the flight attendant was too, because she replied, "Well, sir, I'm sorry, but that's the way the steak is prepared. You're not going to be able to have one cooked another way."

"That's not good enough!" he screamed at her. "I want a new steak!"

The flight attendant stayed calm and again offered to bring him something else.

Then he announced to the plane, "I paid for business class, and this lady won't give me the food I want. How is that for business class?"

"Sir," she said politely, "you wouldn't know business class if it bit you in the rear end."

By the time this skirmish was over, three flight attendants had crowded around the passenger's chair, and I was scared they were going to divert the plane for security concerns.

I didn't say anything out loud, since Cletus was a rather large man, but I did think, *Dude! You are on a plane! In a chair in the air! You are flying to Israel. A hundred years ago, if you'd wanted to go to Israel, you'd have been on a boat and you'd most likely have been attacked by pirates. If you'd managed to survive, you most likely would have gotten scurvy by the time you reached your destination. You're on a plane, watching a movie, eating a steak, and wearing really cool little booties. Shut up and be happy!*

But then I just sat there remembering that I, too, have a choice about how I view life. I can be a Cletus, choosing to be mad about everything, or I can be someone who believes that no matter what happens, God is still God and God is still good.

Most of us tend to believe that God is good when circumstances are going our way but that He isn't so good when things are falling apart. What we need to grasp, however, is that our circumstances do not alter His character.

When we face tough times, one of the questions we must wrestle with is, Are we going to allow our circumstances to determine what we believe about God, or are we going to allow what we believe about God to determine how we handle our circumstances?

> **Our circumstances do not alter His character.**

If we refuse to allow our circumstances to shape what we believe about God, we will walk in freedom from fear, knowing that the One who holds tomorrow is good and is in complete control.

My Redeemer Lives

For years when I'd read the book of Job, I somehow assumed his faith was always rock solid. I thought he never questioned God or doubted what He was doing. And while that seems to be true in the first two chapters, we see more of a roller coaster of faith throughout the rest of the book.

About halfway through the book, we come across what I call the catalyst verses that hold Job's story together.

Whenever Job's friends questioned his standing with God, Job consistently declared his innocence. He essentially said, "If God would come down here and talk to me, I would straighten out this mess with Him" (see Job 13).

And then, sure enough, God offered him this reply:

The LORD answered Job from the whirlwind:

"Who is this that questions my wisdom
    with such ignorant words?
Brace yourself like a man,
      because I have some questions for you,
      and you must answer them."

JOB 38:1-3

Here's my question: if Job was solid in his faith, then why would God have spoken to him like that? It's simple—because Job was human. He doubted. He wrestled. He was angry. He had questions. He struggled with God's goodness . . . just as all of us do.

Jesus once said that John the Baptist was the greatest man who ever lived (see Matthew 11:11). In fact, John was the first person to openly acknowledge Jesus: "The next day John saw Jesus coming toward him and said, 'Look! The Lamb of God who takes away the sin of the world!'" (John 1:29).

But later in his life, John the Baptist struggled to accept who Jesus really was. When John the Baptist was in prison, he kept hearing a lot of stories about Jesus, so he sent his friends to ask Jesus, "Are you the Messiah we've been expecting, or should we keep looking for someone else?" (Matthew 11:2-3).

How does *that* happen? How do you go from "Look, the Lamb of God" to "Are you really the one?"

It's simple: John's circumstances changed. He went from having a crowd of followers to being a prisoner on death row, and as a result he wrestled with doubt. And if the person Jesus called the greatest had his doubts, then you and I will too.

In the midst of his doubts and pain, Job makes this incredible statement:

As for me, I know that my Redeemer lives,
   and he will stand upon the earth at last.
And after my body has decayed,
   yet in my body I will see God!
I will see him for myself.
    Yes, I will see him with my own eyes.
    I am overwhelmed at the thought!

JOB 19:25-27

Job had lost his children, his fortune, and his health. His marriage was falling apart, and his friends were blaming him for his troubles. And yet in the middle of it all, he says that he knows God is alive, that he will one day see Him, and that he refuses to give up on Him.

As followers of Jesus, we base our hope not on our circumstances but rather on the truths that God is God and God is good! No matter what happens, no matter what comes our way, we can walk in victory. We know that the One we follow faced the most overwhelming circumstances this world could have thrown at Him, and three days later, He proved once and for all that nothing could hold Him down.

If Jesus is in you, then nothing can hold you down either.

All Things for Good

One of the most misunderstood verses in the Bible is Romans 8:28: "We know that God causes everything to work together for the good of those who love God and are called according to his purpose for them."

I've heard many well-meaning people try to use that verse to claim that God works everything for good as we define it.

You may be tempted to argue, "Well, I'm not seeing anything good." The reason you can't see the good is because God isn't finished! When He's done, you *will* see the good.

How do you think Job felt at the end of chapter 2, after he lost almost everything that mattered to him? I'm sure he was completely overwhelmed!

But we can stand back and find comfort in the book of Job because we've read chapter 42. We know how the story ends: "The LORD blessed Job in the second half of his life even more than in the beginning" (verse 12).

We can't see God being good and sovereign when we are in the middle of pain. However, if you feel like Job in chapter 2, then hold on—chapter 42 is on the way. In chapter 2 we want to give up, but in chapter 42 we want to throw up our hands in worship because we're in awe that God can take our tragic situation and turn it into something amazing.

I've had people say to me, "I just don't see how God can turn my overwhelming circumstances into something good." I understand the feeling, and I've been there myself. But this is the same God who turned a crucifixion into a resurrection, a bloodstained cross into an empty tomb. And if He did it then, He can do it again. He's the same God!

When I've wrestled with doubts about God's goodness in the past, one of my biggest temptations has been to tell God what He should have done . . . how He could have changed the outcome or eased the pain or made things less hurtful.

But over time I've realized how arrogant it is to try to advise God.

I'm a huge *Star Wars* fan, and I've seen every movie in the six-part series numerous times. If you were to sit down and watch all six *Star Wars* movies back to back, it would take around thirteen and a half hours (I know—I just googled it!).

So let's say you sat down and watched only fifteen seconds of just one of these movies. That's fifteen seconds of more than thirteen hours' worth of stories. And after watching those fifteen seconds you decided to call George Lucas and tell him you felt like you completely knew the plot of the movie and you wanted to share with him seven ways you feel he could have made the story more compelling.

None of us would dare to say that's a brilliant idea when it comes to George Lucas, but how many times have we attempted the same thing with God?

God is outside of time. He doesn't have our limitations. And because of that, we have to trust that He has our circumstances in His hands. He is working things out to make the end of the story better than what we can see from our limited perspective.

God is the only One in the universe who can use our pain for our progress. Think about it—all those in the Bible we hold up as heroes of the faith had to walk through significant pain to get to a place where God could use them. I've seen in Scripture and in life that our potential to be blessed by God comes in direct proportion to the pain we are willing to endure.

> **God is the only One in the universe who can use our pain for our progress.**

Stay with me here. Let's say I go to the doctor today and he tells me I have cancer. Then, after informing me about my problem, he produces a scalpel and says, "We need to cut it out of you."

How insane would it be if I said, "You're a horrible doctor! If you loved me at all, then you wouldn't wound me!"

If he were a good doctor, he would say, "Actually, it's because I care about you that I'm willing to wound you to remove what will kill you if it remains inside you."

I'm so glad God loves me enough to wound me when necessary in order to remove what would destroy me if left untouched.

And I'm so glad He has been teaching me to define His goodness based on who He is, not on my own limited understanding of Him.

CHAPTER 35

GOD IS
NOT SILENT

Being a father has taught me a lot about myself. One of the significant things I've discovered since my daughter was born is that I'm capable of levels of frustration I never thought possible. If you're a parent, I'm sure you can relate—I'm guessing there have been times when you, too, have been completely frustrated by your children.

Like when you're speeding down the road and they ask you how fast you're going.

Or when they start asking questions . . . and three hours later they're still going.

Or when you go into the bathroom to get away for just a few minutes, and before you know it, you see little hands under the door. There's no escaping the voice shouting, "What are you doing in there?"

However, one of the most frustrating things for a parent is to watch your kids give up on something you know they can do. It simply breaks your heart to see them quit when they are capable of so much more.

When Charisse was learning how to ride her bike, it was difficult for me to watch, because I knew she could do it and I knew she was going to love it once she got the hang of it. But every time she faced a setback, she wanted to quit.

I believe that's how our heavenly Father feels about us. He knows what we can do, and He doesn't want us to give up.

He knows we're frustrated.

He knows we're tired.

He knows we're struggling.

He knows we want to quit because we are in chapter 2. But chapter 42 is coming—and it's a lot closer than we think.

He knows how things will turn out.

One of our biggest struggles when we're going through tough times is the apparent silence of God. As we read the story of Job, God is seemingly silent in chapters 3–37. Without knowing the rest of the story, we might make the assumption that since God is silent, He doesn't care or He's not able to do anything to help.

But just because God is silent, that doesn't mean He's absent. If we want to be blessed by God, like Job was in chapter 42, then we can't give up.

The apostle Paul also writes about the need to keep an eternal perspective.

> That is why we never give up. Though our bodies are dying,
> our spirits are being renewed every day. For our present
> troubles are small and won't last very long. Yet they produce for
> us a glory that vastly outweighs them and will last forever! So
> we don't look at the troubles we can see now; rather, we fix our
> gaze on things that cannot be seen. For the things we see now
> will soon be gone, but the things we cannot see will last forever.
> 2 CORINTHIANS 4:16-18

Notice that Paul says our present troubles are small.

But they don't feel that way, do they? They feel overwhelming! You might say to Paul, "You can't say that about my situation!"

But let's take a look at Paul's life. He was beaten multiple times. He was stoned (the old-fashioned way, not the way made popular in the 1960s) and left for dead. His boat was shipwrecked. He was falsely accused of crimes he never committed. Yet here he says that the troubles of this world are small and that something greater is on the way.

When we go through tough times, the battle we face is to take our focus off our circumstances, because Jesus is greater than whatever we're going through. We should stop asking, "Why am I going through this?" and begin asking, "God, what do you want to teach me through this?"

Double the Blessings

We don't know all the specifics about how God blessed Job's life, but the Bible does give us a glimpse.

To begin with, God blessed Job by giving him more material possessions than he had lost. At the beginning of the book we read about what he started out with: "He owned 7,000 sheep, 3,000 camels, 500 teams of oxen, and 500 female donkeys. He also had many servants. He was, in fact, the richest person in that entire area" (Job 1:3). Then the end of the book records that God blessed Job with twice as much as he'd possessed before: "Now he had 14,000 sheep, 6,000 camels, 1,000 teams of oxen, and 1,000 female donkeys" (Job 42:12).

I'm not a math expert, but it seems that God doubled what Job had lost.

Job had some major issues with his friends during his suffering too, as they attacked and criticized him for his lack of faith. But in the end, he gets divine justice:

> After the LORD had finished speaking to Job, he said to Eliphaz the Temanite: "I am angry with you and your two friends, for you have not spoken accurately about me, as my servant Job has. So take seven bulls and seven rams and go to my servant Job and offer a burnt offering for yourselves. My servant Job will pray for you, and I will accept his prayer on your behalf. I will not treat you as you deserve, for you have not spoken accurately about me, as my servant Job has." So Eliphaz the Temanite, Bildad the Shuhite, and Zophar the Naamathite did

as the LORD commanded them, and the LORD accepted Job's prayer.

JOB 42:7-9

God intervened in those relationships, and things were made right. God didn't allow Job to become bitter at his friends, and He made sure the relationships were salvaged.

God also restored Job's family. After losing all his children in chapter 1, Job is eventually blessed with more children: "He also gave Job seven more sons and three more daughters" (Job 42:13). And while those new children could never replace the ones he'd lost, that new family was a tangible sign of God's faithfulness. "Job lived 140 years after that, living to see four generations of his children and grandchildren" (Job 42:16).

> **Don't give up on the God who has never given up on you!**

And it kind of goes without saying, but if Job had that many kids, he and Mrs. Job must have worked through their issues and built an even stronger marriage than before.

God restored and blessed Job in every area of his life. And if He did that for Job, then He can do it for you.

The One Who Never Quit

I wish I could say I've never struggled with wanting to quit—believing my best days are behind me and there's no need to proceed forward.

I remember a day not too long ago when I was simply overwhelmed with life.

It wasn't one big thing but rather a hundred little things that had all piled up on me and had me wanting to give up.

Then I talked with a friend who spoke the truth to me in love, and his words still stick with me today.

When I told him I wanted to quit, he looked me in the eye and said, "Don't do it!"

I asked him to give me one good reason why I shouldn't throw in the towel, and he said, "Because one day we're going to stand in front of the One whose assignment was much tougher than ours. He was betrayed, attacked, and beaten, and He suffered beyond anything we can imagine. And He is the One we follow. If He didn't quit, then neither should you."

God is greater than what you're going through . . . so don't give up on the God who has never given up on you!

THE WEIGHT OF THE WORLD

Recently I was in my basement lifting weights.

For the past two decades, I've tried to make a consistent habit of taking care of myself physically. I do a mixture of cardio and weight lifting, and normally I'm smart about how much I lift, especially since I do my lifting alone.

However, that particular day was an exception—not to mention proof of my stupidity.

I remember feeling good that morning—*really* good. For some reason the amount I usually bench-pressed felt like no challenge at all.

I don't know if I'd had an extra cup of coffee that morning or if I'd slept really well the night before, but for whatever reason, I was throwing weights around my basement like someone training for the Olympics.

Then I had "the thought."

What if I tried lifting more today?

It made sense. I'd been feeling awesome all morning and had no reason to doubt I could handle more weight.

Looking back, I suppose there was a still, small voice in my mind telling me that what I was about to do was really not a good idea, but

I chose to ignore it. I loaded way more weight on the bar than I was used to.

After all, no pain, no gain, right?

I lay down on the bench and lifted the weight off the rack.

Yep, it felt a lot heavier, but I was strong. I knew I could handle it. My goal was to do three reps at that weight.

The first rep was tough, but I managed to touch my chest and push the bar up.

The second time was way more challenging, and I began to think that maybe this wasn't such a great idea.

I should have quit at that point, put the weight back on the rack, and called it a win. But whether because of ignorance, pride, or a combination of the two, I kept going.

I brought the weight down, touched the bar to my chest, and began to push it up again. It was at this point that my chest informed me it was done, and the weight came crashing down on me.

Now I was in what you would refer to as a helpless situation.

No one else was home. And even if Lucretia and Charisse had been there, they wouldn't have been able to get the weight off me.

I couldn't get to my phone to call someone.

I was, to put it mildly, *overwhelmed*.

It took a while, but I finally managed to get out from under the pressure of the weight. It was an excruciating experience. But as I look back, I can see so many parallels between my own life and that fateful day of weight lifting.

For one thing, sometimes I think I can handle certain things that are too heavy for me. We've all been there—we encounter a situation and think, *No big deal; I can handle it.*

But then the unexpected happens, and the situation we saw as manageable comes crashing down on us. That's because life is cumulative. What we thought wasn't a big deal may not be, in and of itself; however, when we throw it in with everything else we're facing, it can be the final thing that makes us lose our grip.

When we get in that type of situation, we don't need a consultant to come along and analyze our problem, nor do we need a theologian to lecture us about our problem. We need someone who will grab the weight off our chest and deliver us from our problem.

Which leads to the next thing I learned from my weight lifting adventure: ask for help!

Looking back on some of my not-so-bright moments, I know I could have avoided a lot of pain if I hadn't tried to lift so much alone.

If I'd had someone with me in the basement that day, he could have helped me realize that it wasn't a wise idea to attempt a third repetition. Or if I did attempt it and failed, he could have helped me get the weight off my chest and saved me a lot of pain.

One of the most powerful lies the enemy will whisper to you in your darkest times is that you are all alone—that no one wants to hear what you are going through and you should just give up.

But life isn't meant to be lived alone! Even Jesus didn't do life alone.

If you're struggling with anxiety, fear, worry, and doubt, you need to understand a few things:

You are not the only one who has had to battle this tough situation.

You are not a bad person because you're going through this.

You are not a lesser human being because you're struggling with this, even if it seems like other people seem to conquer the same situation with no problem.

And most important, in Christ you are defined by being His son or daughter, not by what you're going through. Even though the storm you are experiencing is intense, He is greater than your storm.

My hope and prayer for you as we close this book is that you will have a greater view of God, a greater understanding of His love and power, and a greater desire to step beyond what has overwhelmed you.

Jesus walked out of a grave as proof to us that we can walk out of what is holding us down.

The weight that is pressing down on you doesn't have to define you, because no matter what you're facing right now . . .

Jesus is greater than your biggest doubt.

Jesus is greater than your deepest regret.

Jesus is greater than your impossible situation.

Jesus is greater than your most overwhelming circumstances.

The empty tomb is proof that nothing can hold Jesus back. And if He lives in you, nothing can hold you back either!

ACKNOWLEDGMENTS

There are so many people I'd like to thank who have helped this book come together. I'm going to try to list most of them!

Thank you to Lucretia and Charisse, for all the time you allowed me to work on this book.

Thanks to the "dream team" I get to work with every single day—Ali, Erin, Sarah, Sarah (yes, there are two Sarahs!), Hykeng, Margie, Annie, and Lindsay. Y'all are amazing!

Thanks to the leadership team I get to serve with at NewSpring Church—Shane, Paul, Brad, Jason, Jason (yes, there are two Jasons), and Michael. I am so glad that Jesus called us to serve Him together.

Thanks to everyone at NewSpring Church—you guys are amazing! One hundred thousand is on the way!

Thank to Clayton and Steven for standing by me and taking my phone calls when I was at the deepest point of my depression. You guys are amazing!

Thanks to John Walker, the best counselor on the planet. The Lord used you to save my life, marriage, and ministry.

Thanks to Sealy for bringing me to the dance.

Thanks to Tyndale for believing in me enough to give me a shot at writing.

Thanks to Stephanie, who worked for hours and hours to help me edit this book. You are awesome!

NOTES

1. I preached an entire message on the topic of depression at our church a couple of years ago. It was, hands down, the most viewed message on our website last year. You can listen to the message here: http://newspring.cc/watch/overwhelmed/win-the-battle-with-depression.
2. L. A. Pratt, D. J. Brody, and Q. Gu, "Antidepressant Use in Persons Aged 12 and Over: United States, 2005–2008," NCHS Data Brief, no. 76, Centers for Disease Control and Prevention, October 2011, http://www.cdc.gov/nchs/data/databriefs/db76.htm.
3. "Porn Profits: Corporate America's Secret," *ABC News*, January 28, 2013, http://abcnews.go.com/Primetime/story?id=132001&page=.

ABOUT THE AUTHOR

Perry Noble is the author of *Unleash!: Breaking Free from Normalcy* and the founding and senior pastor of NewSpring Church, which was rated #2 on the Outreach 100 America's Fastest-Growing Churches list in 2013. His primary concerns are being a servant to Jesus Christ; a husband to his wife, Lucretia; and a father to their daughter, Charisse. Perry is also passionate about seeing people meet Jesus, leading his church staff, and pouring himself into other church leaders on a local and global level. You can find him online at www.perrynoble.com.

PRAISE FOR
PERRY NOBLE'S
UNLEASH!

"Perry knows the power of living an unleashed life, and now you can too. I am delighted to recommend his book to you. It will challenge you to be all you can be!"

JOHN C. MAXWELL, AUTHOR AND SPEAKER

"This book will give you hope that the powerful grace of God is really and truly available to you in Jesus Christ."

MARK DRISCOLL, FOUNDING PASTOR OF MARS HILL CHURCH, COFOUNDER OF THE ACTS 29 NETWORK, AND #1 *NEW YORK TIMES* BESTSELLING AUTHOR

"I love this book! Each chapter is chock-full of practical wisdom you can immediately apply to experience a breakthrough in areas you thought could never change."

RICK WARREN, PASTOR OF SADDLEBACK CHURCH AND *NEW YORK TIMES* BESTSELLING AUTHOR OF *THE PURPOSE DRIVEN LIFE*

"Perry Noble is a man of unswerving and uncompromising faith in God. He has turned that passion to the page to help us all learn how to leave normal behind and live a life unleashed."

STEVEN FURTICK, LEAD PASTOR OF ELEVATION CHURCH AND AUTHOR OF *SUN STAND STILL*

"Perry Noble is one of the most gifted communicators I know. I am blessed to know Perry, and you will be blessed by the message the Lord has given him."

ROBERT MORRIS, SENIOR PASTOR OF GATEWAY CHURCH AND BESTSELLING AUTHOR OF *THE BLESSED LIFE, FROM DREAM TO DESTINY,* AND *THE GOD I NEVER KNEW*

"If you're tired of doing things halfway and are ready to experience God's power in a new way, you are ready for *Unleash!*"

CRAIG GROESCHEL, SENIOR PASTOR OF LIFECHURCH.TV AND AUTHOR OF *SOUL DETOX*

CP0736

UNLEASH!
PERRY NOBLE
BREAKING FREE FROM NORMALCY

Jesus promised us a full and abundant life. Perry Noble challenges us in his book "Unleash!" how to grab on to God's promise of full and complete living. You can break free from normalcy and live an unleashed life!

Available in stores and online

WWW.UNLEASHBOOK.COM
#UNLEASHBOOK

NewSpring
CHURCH

NewSpring Church exists to reach people far from God and teach them to follow Jesus step by step. With campuses all across the state of South Carolina, NewSpring Church is on a mission to reach 100,000 people for Christ.

Visit our website for more information and for resources you can use to overcome feeling overwhelmed.

www.newspring.cc

CP0743

A GIFT FOR
YOU

To help you during times of feeling Overwhelmed, we would love to offer you an Overwhelmed Stress Reliever Ball. Visit OverwhelmedBook.com to order. The only charge is $2 to cover the cost of shipping and handling.

www.OverwhelmedBook.com
#OverwhelmedBook

CP0744